Since the beginning of written [illegible] been a marvelous teaching tool [illegible] tion, and guidance for His people. This is certainly true with Steve Wingfield's new work. I could hardly stop reading, completed the compilation in one day. God shows HIS power through these FAITH STORIES to help each reader understand His power as Creator. When He touches our lives with individual situations, He lets us know He is daily in charge of big things as well, always there for His children. Our brother, Steve, has shown this, especially so in the Romanian faith story that so touches one's heart, seeing how the greatest of evil can be overcome by the greatest of good, often with tears in my eyes. I recommend this work heartily to anyone who has a desire to be so touched. God at work.

—Tom Phillips
Billy Graham Evangelistic Association, Senior Advisor, Will Graham

Steve came to faith at Thomas Road Baptist Church in 1970 and his life has been an adventure of faith ever since. I pray this book will encourage your faith walk.

—Jonathan Falwell
Pastor, Thomas Road Baptist Church and
Chancellor of Liberty University

This book will inspire your faith journey! It is one thing to talk about living by faith, and it is another to actually live it! Steve "walks the talk" as he lives by faith, and this book inspired me and encouraged me in my own faith journey. I need a regular healthy dose of heroes like Steve who model what it looks like to live every day 100% devoted to the gospel. The stories you will read will propel your faith journey forward just as Steve's life example has springboarded a renewal of my own faith as we serve God together at the Lodestar Mountain Inn. May Steve's faith journey impact your life like it has mine!

—Josh Beers
President, OneLife Institute

I've known Steve since his first pastorate in Roanoke. During—and since—those years, his passion has been on evangelism and discipleship. I owe much of my walk of faith to his early-morning discipleship studies. This book is a reflection of that passion. That kind of lifelong ministry can only come from complete allegiance to Jesus and His command 'to go into all the world and make disciples.' The trip to Romania was a life-changing experience for me but more, an example of Steve's willingness to take sometimes seemingly risky ventures for the sake of proclaiming the gospel of our Lord. I pray that God will continue to bless Steve and the entire ministry team.

—Bill Overstreet

I was born and raised Amish. I left home when I was 16, traveled, and became a successful businessman. Although I always believed in God, I never worshipped Him until I was baptized by Steve. Since then, I cannot live without God. Everything and anything I do is God's will. I am grateful to Steve.

—Bob Detweiler

Probably one of the hardest things for a preacher to teach is faith. Steve has taught me faith through his leadership and his commitment to God.

—Brandon Traylor

Steve Wingfield is a master storyteller. If you read this with the right inflection, and know when to pause for laughter, it'll feel like you're sitting around a campfire with my dad as the stars wink overhead.

—David Wingfield

With over fifty years in ministry and forty-plus years as a senior pastor, I can never share my faith story without mentioning Steve Wingfield and the tremendous role he played in leading me to a personal faith in Jesus Christ. Steve has truly been a brother in the Lord and a mentor in ministry for these fifty-plus years. This book will touch your heart and challenge your walk of faith. My prayer is that each of us will by faith first 'set the table' and then see what the Lord has in store for us.

—Dr. Don L. Paxton

I have known Steve since 1973. First, when he would stop in at Stoltzfus Farm Restaurant on Saturday evenings to pick up Barb for a date. That same year, he spoke at the farm, at a tent meeting titled "Key '73." Julie and I had the honor and privilege to serve on his board, and I have traveled with Steve to Romania, when it was nearly impossible to enter the country under the rule of Ceauşescu.

It's been an honor and blessing to work with Steve in missions and evangelism. Our friendship is a gift I treasure greatly. As the stories in this book prove, Steve is a man of God, walks his talk, and practices what he preaches. His message remains the same: "Jesus Christ is Lord." This book is the encouragement we need to tell others about our Savior, Jesus Christ.

—Ike Stoltzfus

As a person walks his or her journey through life, his or her faith can be challenged. I found *Faith Stories* to be an excellent tool to build my faith.

—Jeff Bowers

My dad is a captivating storyteller. For over four decades, I've watched people gathered around a table, in church pews, or standing in an outdoor venue listening to my dad. *I* never get tired of hearing him, and *he* never gets tired of telling stories and relaying the Greatest Story of all time. But I have wondered how one person could have the range of adventures that my dad has and how one Christian could consistently encounter people ready to say Yes! to the good news of Jesus. Faith and faithfulness are the secret sauce, I believe. For an imperfect man, my dad is remarkably faithful to engage with the people he meets and to ask questions that can open eyes and hearts to God's work. That must be why God keeps setting him up with more inspiring "faith stories" like these.

—**Michelle Wingfield Curlin**

In this book, Steve Wingfield does a beautiful job of depicting how God chooses ordinary men, and then transforms them into useful tools to achieve amazing things for his glory. Steve interweaves these miraculous stories of faith in a manner that clearly demonstrates God's power to achieve his purposes *and* transform broken vessels into ambassadors for Jesus Christ, that Author and Finisher of our salvation.

—**Pete Lulusa**

It is almost unfathomable to think that Jesus Christ the Creator of everything, seen or unseen, can be taken by surprise. And yet, He was. He was pleasantly surprised by the faith of people from the unexpected corners of Jewish society, the Roman officer of the occupational force—the most hated people in all Israel, and the despised and unclean Canaanite woman of Syrophoenician territory.

Faith is one of the most precious pearls that Jesus was looking for. And it was not found in the Temple of Jerusalem with high priests, nor in the prestigious seminary of Jewish Academy with professor emeritus Gamaliel, nor among the highest religious strata of religious elites, but in "the little people" who seem so far away from the heritage of Abraham.

"You need to be one to see one." The evangelist Steve Wingfield learned very well from the Master. In his national and international ministries he was looking through the eyes of Jesus to discover that hidden pearl in the hearts of the people. This book will inspire you today to live in such a way that will surprise not only the people around you but even Jesus Christ.

Nothing is more important in his life than to live for the greatest encounter at the Golden Gate of heaven and be greeted by Jesus Himself with these words: "Well done, good and faithful slave. You were faithful with a few things, I will put you in charge of many things; enter the joy of your master."

—Titus Coltea

I was arrested and deported from Romania in 1988 for preaching the gospel. My heart broke because I loved the Romanian people. God was working mightily in the country. I asked Steve Wingfield if he would take my place in meetings that I had scheduled to take place a few months later. Steve took a giant step of faith and went to Romania.

And, oh, how God blessed his faith. He became a wonderful instrument in the hands of God during the revolution and afterward. How I thank God for Steve's faith. I'm so glad that he has recorded this and many other stories of faith. They will encourage you. Every great work for God is done by faith. These stories will strengthen your faith and place you on the road to seeing God do great things.

—Sammy Tippit

Steve's journey of unshakable faith in life is a testament of his calling in life. Few people have the courage to keep on keeping on when things don't go as planned. As a result, there will be thousands of people who have an eternal future in heaven because of his willingness to share the gospel anywhere at any time with anyone. These stories will inspire all who read them and will increase our awareness that we are all called to spread the good news wherever we go. His enthusiasm is contagious.

—Paul Weaver

I first met Steve Wingfield in the summer of 1971. We'd had a special day at Thomas Road Baptist Church, and Steve invited 51 people who accepted his invitation to be in attendance. I knew then that God had called him to be an evangelist. His life has exhibited faith in so many ways. We have prayed together every Sunday morning for almost 40 years. We missed a few because of international travel, but very few. I always look forward to a time for prayer or to exercise faith and believe God for even greater things. God will use this book in your life. May you be motivated to exercise the faith that God has given you.

—Dr. Elmer Towns

Inspired! *Faith Stories* moves one's heart to trust in the Lord Jesus Christ. Steve Wingfield has penned what he has lived. The stories contained in this book are not only true and faithful to the call of God on Steve's life but also deeply inspiring. Thanks, Steve, for putting on paper what you have shared with many of us in stories throughout the years. Young reader take note! These are not fairy tales or fables from a book of make-believe. These are stories of true faith in our recent history. These are stories to read and remember. Mark your mind and heart with the working of God through the life of one man, evangelist, who will believe and follow God no matter the cost. As the Bible says, "without faith it is impossible to please God" (Hebrews 11:6). Or, as Paul said, "I can do all things through Christ who strengthens me" (Philippians 4:13). Read, remember, and believe!

—Tim Robnett
DMin, President, ETeamGlobal

I've known Steve for several years now. He is one of the few people working actively to help introduce people to Jesus at the racetrack. It has been my privilege to speak at his Victory Weekend events at NASCAR tracks. Steve's faith is nothing short of inspirational. It is such a blessing to spend time with him and experience his energy and passion to reach people for Christ. I pray this book will motivate you to exercise your faith.

—Josh Reaume
owner/driver of Reaume Brothers Racing

FAITH
STORIES

STEVE WINGFIELD

BROOKSTONE
PUBLISHING GROUP
Birmingham, Alabama

Faith Stories

Brookstone Publishing Group
An imprint of Iron Stream Media
100 Missionary Ridge
Birmingham, AL 35242
IronStreamMedia.com

Copyright © 2023 by Steve Wingfield

Library of Congress Control Number: 2023904350

Cover design by Hannah Linder Designs

ISBN: 978-1-960814-00-5 (paperback)
ISBN: 978-1-960814-01-2 (eBook)

1 2 3 4 5—26 25 24 23 22

CONTENTS

FOREWORD

~

I'm always encouraged and inspired when I get to sit down for coffee or lunch with a friend or family member and hear how God is working in their life. And that's the experience I had reading Steve's book. It's personal. It's challenging. It's refreshing. Through his journey from America to Romania and all around the world, through the struggles and the victories, it's clear that God moved mightily when Steve listened to His voice. The stories in this book show me the truth of Hebrews 11:1: "Faith is the assurance of things hoped for, the conviction of things not seen." There is reality and evidence of Steve's faith and God's faithfulness. What you'll clearly see is:

- God's hand on Steve's life—from his rejection of God to his life of faith in Christ; from business to ministry.
- God's hand on Steve's family and friends—from his son, David, to his friend in communist Romania, Pete Lulusa.
- God's hand on Steve's ministry—from revival meetings to Lodestar Mountain Inn to OneLife.

These stories give me the strength and confidence to live out my faith more fully. I want to shout, "It's true! It's true! Our faith makes a difference! The evidence and reality can be seen—in a life devoted to Jesus!"

Kathy Price
Steve's pastor's wife

– 1 –

FAITH: A WAY OF LIFE

~~

When Floyd Wingfield was a young boy, he was called of God to go into the ministry. He was sure of the call, but for many years, it looked like he'd never be able to answer that call.

Floyd was my father. My grandfather died in the pandemic of 1918, and my dad quit school as a twelve-year-old boy and went to work doing a man's job to help support the family. At seventeen, he and my mom were married. He worked at the shoe factory in Lynchburg, Virginia, for a period of time and then bought a farm in Rustburg, Virginia.

By the time I came along, the Wingfield family already had six children. When I was born, I had a twenty-two-year-old sister, a twenty-year-old sister, an eighteen-year-old brother, a fifteen-year-old brother, and twin brothers who were ten. My mom said I wasn't planned but I was always wanted.

Finally, when I was six months old, Dad answered that call he had been given when he was a boy. He was assigned to four little Methodist churches in Bedford County, Virginia, and we moved to the foothills of the Blue Ridge Mountains, to a small town called Huddleston.

These were the days when they "pounded" the preacher. Each spring and fall, everybody would bring a pound of this and a pound of that for the preacher's family so we'd have food to eat. There were times when the cupboard was almost empty. At a family reunion about ten years ago, I heard the story of one day when the pantry was completely bare.

Our family came home from church that Sunday and my dad asked, "Honey, what's for dinner?"

"Floyd, we don't have anything for dinner," replied Mom. "The cupboard's bare. I don't even have food for the baby." (That would have been me. My mom was forty-four when I was born, and she was not producing enough milk to feed me.)

Dad said, "Set the table, honey."

"Floyd," she repeated, "we don't have anything to eat."

He said, "Set the table."

Mom set the table and the family sat down around it. Dad prayed and thanked God for the food we had to eat.

As he was praying, a gentleman he had led to Christ drove up. This man had a little country store, and that day he brought our family milk, potatoes, bread, flour, canned beans, ham, roast beef—everything that we needed, plus more!

That's the home in which I was raised. That's the faith that my mom and dad exhibited to me as a way of life. My dad lived what he preached, and it was that living out of faith that left the greatest impression on me.

One day Dad and I were walking on Main Street in Lynchburg, Virginia. I was still pretty young, and it seemed to me that everyone in town knew and greeted "Wink" Wingfield, my dad's nickname.

"Wink," one man said as he met us and stopped to talk, "could you spot me some money for a cup of coffee?"

Even at my age, I could tell this man was in the grip of alcohol addiction. I was wary of him, and I wondered what Dad would say and do.

Dad took out his wallet and opened it; it was empty. Then he pulled out the small change purse he used to carry his coins. He dumped out the contents. Two dimes and a "round tuit" lay in his palm.

He always carried that "round tuit" as a witnessing tool. It was a round piece of wood imprinted with the words *Round Tuit*. When Dad talked with someone about the Lord and attending church, the other person would often say, "Preacher, I'll get there when I get around to it." And then Dad would say, "Well, I've got one right here. I'll give it to you . . ."

We were standing on the sidewalk in front of Texas Tavern as Dad checked the coins in his change purse. Then he pulled open the door of the eatery and walked in, with the man following us. (Texas Tavern is not a beer joint; it's a hamburger-hot dog-chili stand.)

My dad put his two dimes on the counter and said to the server, "Give my buddy a cup of coffee."

To the man who had asked for the coffee, he said, "Jim, you don't have to live like this. God's got better things for you. You need to let Him deliver you from this addiction."

And me? I'm thinking, *I'm hungry! We don't have money. You just gave away everything we had. What am I supposed to do?*

We left and had walked only thirty or so steps when Dad stopped, reached down, and picked up a dollar bill lying on the sidewalk.

"Son," he said, "remember this: You can never outgive God."

My dad not only taught me faith but also taught me to trust God for great things and to be a faithful witness. I saw him live out that faith and witness, not only that day on the sidewalk in Lynchburg but every day of his life. I've tried to live it out in my life as well.

God's been so good, and I thank Him for His goodness. Have faith in Him, my friend. Trust Him in everything. He'll see you through.

– 2 –

FROM "I DON'T WANT TO" TO "I'LL SHARE YOU WITH EVERYONE"

~~~

In the summer of 1969, I had a seasonal job driving a truck for American Tobacco Company. I'd pick up the tobacco at the auction house and take it to their warehouse. The job paid well and I enjoyed it very much, but when the season ended in September, I was looking for something else to do.

I had quit college. What was really going on was that I was running from the Lord. I knew He had called me into ministry, but I didn't want to do it.

Metropolitan Ambulance Service was advertising for an ambulance attendant. *That sounds like an exciting job*, I thought. *I believe I'll apply.* The service had a contract with the city of Lynchburg, and they had just taken over the service of all funeral homes. We did all transportation within the city limits, both emergency and convalescent.

More than seventy-five people applied for the job. I didn't know how to put on a Band-Aid, but for some reason, they hired me. This was before the era of EMTs and paramedics. Basically, we had first-aid training and that was it.

My first week on the job, I was to go to first-aid classes with the Red Cross during the day and at night ride with the ambulances to observe everything that took place. On the first day of my employment, I went to my class and then showed up at work at 4:30 p.m. for my five o'clock shift.

As I walked in the door, everyone was leaving for a three-alarm wreck on the west side of Lynchburg. Only the dispatcher and I were left in the building. We were talking when one of the guys I was going to be working with walked in—and as he did, a woman was hit by a car right in front of our building.

"Come on! Let's go!" he said.

I couldn't drive because I didn't have a chauffeur's license, so I had to ride in the back of the ambulance with the lady who was injured.

"What should I do?" I asked.

The driver said, "Just clean her up a little bit."

She was bleeding, and I didn't know what to do. I opened the first-aid kit and saw some rubbing alcohol. I tried applying that to some gauze—but that didn't work, believe me.

We arrived at the hospital, and just as we drove up to the ER, we got a call about a heart attack victim. We put the injured woman on a stretcher in the ER and rushed back to the ambulance. Heading out, I was in the back, making up the bed as we were on our way to the next call.

I'd never seen a dead person except at a funeral. The man was lying on the floor, his wife was crying, the neighbors were gathered around. My partner put a resuscitator on the man and told me to start heart massage.

This was way beyond my training, but I started rubbing the man's chest.

"Just quit," my partner said. "We need to transport him." Needless to say, the man did not make it.

The job (and my training and skills) got better over time. I actually had a great experience and enjoyed it. In many ways, my employment with the ambulance service was a wonderful time.

But it was also a hellish place for me. I was not following Christ then, and I was surrounded by people who weren't followers of Christ either. Life was full of temptations, like the lure of pornography, and I saw plenty of guys running around on their wives.

During that time, I met many police officers who worked part-time with the ambulance service. Some of them encouraged me to join the police department, so I did. Like them, I divided my time between the police force and the ambulance service. That went on for a year, but the police department was not a good fit for me.

I started looking for another job. Because of my police and ambulance training, I landed a job as a safety investigator at a nuclear power plant just south of Lynchburg. Radiation Control and Industrial Safety operated out of the same office. My responsibility was to look for safety violations and investigate accidents. In the providence of God, the person who was in charge of Radiation Control was a committed follower of Christ.

It was a Wednesday morning in July 1970 when I walked into the office and my friend Bill asked what I was doing that night.

"Nothing," I said.

"Why don't you go to church with me?" They were having special meetings with a guest speaker.

"Bill," I said, "I'm not interested." I hadn't been to church for about a year. I was really into the party scene. Out of respect for my mom and dad and my family, I wasn't living as wildly as I could have been, but I had walked away from faith.

About ten o'clock that morning, we took a coffee break. Bill started up again, talking about this speaker and how good he was and again he said, "I know you would love it."

"Bill, give it up! I'm not going!"

At noon, we went to lunch, and I discovered Bill was hearing impaired. At least, he hadn't heard anything I had said earlier, and he started in again. This time, I was so upset that I said, "Look, just forget it!" and I got up and moved to another table.

About 2:30 that afternoon, he came over to my desk and apologized and asked me to forgive him.

"It's OK," I said.

"Well, I don't want anything to happen to our friendship."

"Bill, our friendship's intact. Everything's OK. I know you mean well," I said.

I was sure I saw tears in his eyes, and he seemed sad. "I . . . just . . . I'm concerned, Steve, and I'd like you to go."

I threw up my hands and said, "OK! I'll meet you there."

"I'll come by and pick you up," he countered.

I have no clue what the man preached on, but he quoted a verse of scripture that has become one of my life verses: John 10:10. Jesus said, "I came that they may have life and have it abundantly" (ESV). That word *abundantly* literally translated from the Greek means "life will be full, meaningful, have purpose and direction."

I sat there thinking about how I could get out of there. I'd heard all that before. My dad was a preacher and so were my brothers. I'd heard this message all my life. I knew I was under conviction, but I just wanted to get out of there and "get my head straight."

But when they sang the hymn of invitation and some people began walking forward, I saw a guy that used to frequent a lot of the same spots I did in Lynchburg. He stepped out and walked down the aisle in response to the invitation.

On July 7, 1970, I said to myself, *If he's got guts enough to do it, I can too.* So I walked forward and surrendered my life to Christ.

That night I gave my life to Christ, but I still did not want to go into the ministry. I knew God had called me, but I did not want to be a preacher.

That night there was a party going on at my apartment and I did not want to be there, so I went home to my parents' house. I waited until they were in bed and I went to my room and went to bed. The next morning my mom was making breakfast and I was sitting at the table talking with her and my dad. I had decided not to tell them about my decision. I was going to wait a few weeks to make sure it took ☺. My mom turned around and said, "What happened to you last night?" I had to tell her the truth. Needless to say, when I told her about giving my life to Christ, she became a shouting Methodist. That is a breakfast I will never forget.

Roy, a friend at the nuclear power plant where I worked, began discipling me, although I didn't realize what he was doing. We were so different; he was a Marine with short hair and white socks. I was not a hippie but, among fundamentalists, my hair was "long." Roy and I were very different, but he had a major impact on my life. He would take me to revival meetings, and I found they were wonderful.

I was addicted to tobacco. Roy walked into my office one day when I was smoking, and I tried to hide my cigarettes. All of a sudden, God convicted me. I put out the cigarette I was smoking, raised my hand, and said, "Lord, I'll never touch another one."

"Praise God!" said Roy. "I've been praying for you."

Roy taught me a great lesson. He didn't get on me about my smoking; he just prayed over it. I'm thankful to God for that. I haven't touched another cigarette since that day. The Lord took away all desire for tobacco.

Later that September I went to church one Wednesday night at Thomas Road Baptist Church and Lester Roloff was preaching. That night, I surrendered my life to ministry.

But I said, "Lord, I'm not going to tell anybody about this. If this is really of You, You are going to have to open the door. This is between me and You."

That was on a Wednesday night. Two days later on Friday night, my dad's church was having special meetings, and I decided I'd go.

Unknown to me, the speaker for the weekend had to leave after the first evening; someone close to him had died. Several of the church leaders had seen such a change in my life that they went to my dad and said, "Why don't we have Steve preach Saturday night and Sunday night, and we'll have a youth emphasis?"

My dad just said, "Go talk to him."

Only two days before, I had promised the Lord that I'd give my life to ministry if He opened the door. So when they asked me to preach, I said, "Yes, I'll do it."

The announcement was made Friday night that I would be preaching Saturday and Sunday nights. I stayed up half that night trying to find something to preach on. The next morning, I was driving around, praying and asking the Lord to speak to me.

I drove to Lynchburg and went into the Baptist bookstore where I browsed the shelves. I guess I was hoping something would jump off the shelf and become my sermon. I did find an album (an LP record) of Billy Graham preaching two sermons and I bought it. Side one was a sermon on Samson. I took it home and listened to it. I said, "That was pretty good." I listened to it again. As I played it the third time, I wrote down an outline.

That night, I preached on Samson using Billy Graham's message and there were twenty-six first-time decisions for Christ. On Sunday afternoon, I listened to the other side, and that sermon was on the Second Coming of Christ, so that's what I preached on Sunday night. Again there was another great response.

Word got around, and I started getting invitations to preach and do youth revivals. I found another sermon somewhere, and God honored that.

I once had the opportunity to tell Dr. Graham the story of my first two sermons, and he said, "Praise God! There's power in His Word!"

Those were my first sermons. It's been a wonderful journey ever since. I love serving the Lord, and I'm thankful to God for all He has done in and through me in spite of all my weaknesses and failures. I figured out a long time ago that if the Lord could use a donkey to talk for Him, I'm home free.

– 3 –

AFTER I ANSWERED THE CALL

~

I had applied to Asbury College and had been accepted, but my brother Wayne was pastoring a church near Harrisonburg, Virginia, and suggested I come up and look at Eastern Mennonite College. I did, and I met Dr. Myron Augsburger, who offered me the opportunity to be his youth evangelist. He was president of the college, but he was also doing crusades. I accepted the youth evangelist position and went to Eastern Mennonite.

I had money saved up for my first year at EMC, but after that year, I needed a job for the summer. The only position that opened up was back with the ambulance service. The owner was going to be gone quite a bit that summer, and he wanted me to manage the service while he was gone. I really didn't want to go back because they knew the old Steve. I remember kneeling beside my bed in my dorm room and praying, "Lord, if that's where You want me, I will go and share You with every person there."

Nineteen people worked at the ambulance service. Some were new hires; some I already knew. I started work at the end of May. By July, I had shared the gospel with every one of them, but nobody had made a decision for Christ.

Don Paxton was the most boisterous of the employees and gave me the hardest time of anybody there, but we were good friends. We were making a convalescent call one day, and I noticed that Don was very quiet.

I said, "What's going on?"

"Oh, nothing," he began, but then he added, "I need Christ."

The night before, Don had been asking me all kinds of questions about God and faith. I thought some of them were kind of crazy, and I had said, "Don, if you're trying to embarrass me, you can do it because I haven't been a Christian that long myself. But I know that I know that Christ has saved me. If you really want an answer to your questions, I know somebody who can answer them."

Now Don knew he needed Christ. After our call, I took my friend to Dr. J. O. Grooms, who was the outreach pastor at Thomas Road Baptist Church. Dr. Grooms and Don talked about salvation, and Don prayed to receive Christ. He came out to the ambulance where I was waiting and praying. When he walked out the door I knew he was a changed man. I started weeping and beating on the steering wheel of the ambulance, rejoicing over what God had done.

There were about six of us that slept in the bunkhouse of the ambulance service to answer calls at night. There were a few nights (very few) when we could sleep all night. That night we went to bed and Don was so excited about Jesus saving him that he started laughing. When asked why he was laughing, he shouted, "I am saved!" He and I got out of bed and were praying together, and soon two other men also got out of bed and came and knelt beside us and prayed to receive Christ. It was wonderful.

So now there were four of us Christians at the ambulance service, and I knew I had to do a Bible study with them. I had not done much follow-up of new believers at that point in my life. I just knew I needed to get them established in the Word because I was going back to school at the end of August. I asked them what they wanted to study and they all said, "The book of Revelation." I didn't know any more than they did, but we all knew we wanted to live for the Lord.

August came and I went back to school. One evening in the middle of September I was studying in the library and the librarian came and said, "You've got a long-distance phone call."

It was my friend Don, and he said, "Steve, pray! Revival's broken out at the ambulance service. The owner got saved, his wife got saved, and it's just awesome."

When I came home for Thanksgiving, the ambulance service had been transformed by Christ! They had planned a special Thanksgiving banquet and asked me to speak. Nineteen people worked at the ambulance service, and eighteen of them had prayed to receive Christ. It was a totally transformed environment; they were handing out gospel literature and playing gospel music in the building—it was just awesome.

Police officers and fire and rescue personnel were also invited to the Thanksgiving banquet. We were setting up for the banquet that night when number nineteen called. Don and I went to his house and prayed with him and his wife to receive Christ.

All nineteen! Revival came to the ambulance service, and lives were transformed. Today, five of those nineteen (I'm one of them) are ministers of the gospel.

It was a miracle of God and a glorious testimony of His faithfulness in using people to tell others about Jesus—using even somebody who didn't know very much but who said, "I am available and I will go where you want me to go." Like Isaiah, I said, "Here am I. Send me!" (Isaiah 6:8 NASB). I have tried to live a life of obedience, and even when I did not know how it was going to work, I have rested in the assurance that He will provide, and He has!

– 4 –

"Ask Him, Dad"

~

It was the week after Christmas, 1984. We were living in the Chicago area where I was completing additional graduate work at Trinity Evangelical Divinity School in the School of World Missions and Evangelism. We were enjoying our Christmas vacation very much as a family. It provided a relief from the academic pressure, and also some time off from my weekend travel as an evangelist.

We decided we could not travel to Pennsylvania and Virginia to visit family and friends for Christmas, so my wife's parents decided to visit us in Chicago. Our two children, Michelle and David, were especially excited about a visit from Grandpa and Grandma. David would be five on December 30, so they would be there to help celebrate his birthday. Michelle (who was seven) and David wanted to take Grandpa and Grandma into downtown Chicago and show them some of their favorite spots. This was to be a very important part of our Christmas celebration, so the children planned the trip with great care.

One important part of the plan was that we must take the commuter train rather than drive. This was fun, but it also meant that once we arrived in the city, we needed to take taxis to various spots of interest.

I must say at this point that we as a family were committed to the task of world evangelization. We tried to practice this as a lifestyle and it was very much a way of life in our home. Consequently,

Michelle and David had observed this lifestyle as the norm of Christian experience. They had both observed Barbara and me sharing our faith on numerous occasions.

Our first trip after arriving in the city was to the Shedd Aquarium. When we got into the taxi, I was in the front seat and Barbara, Michelle, David, and Barbara's parents were in the back seat.

I began a conversation with the driver but was not getting to the main point as quickly as David remembered I should. David leaned over the front seat and whispered, "Ask him, Dad." I said that I would and continued to involve the driver in conversation.

Then David said, "Dad, ask him if he is a Christian."

The driver heard David and said, "Praise the Lord, brother!"

As it turned out, the driver was a pastor in the inner city and drove taxi part time. This was a great encouragement to David.

Later that morning, we entered a second taxi. Almost before I could tell the driver where we wanted to go, David leaned over the front seat and said, "Dad, ask him if he's a Christian."

The driver said, "Me Christian." He was from Korea and was studying at the University of Chicago. He was actually a member of the world's largest church in Seoul, Korea.

Our third driver was quite different. He appeared to be in his sixties and to have lived a very difficult life. David again said, "Dad, ask him if he's a Christian."

The driver heard the question, looked in the rearview mirror, and replied, "I'm an agnostic."

David looked at me and asked, "What's that, Dad?"

My reply was, "He believes there is a God, but he doesn't think God can do anything to help him."

"Well, Jesus could save him," David said.

"Yes, David, if he would only ask, Jesus could save him."

Things were quiet until we reached our destination. Everyone got out of the car, and I prepared to pay the driver.

"Mister, I don't want your money," he said. "You all are Christians, and I want to do this to help you."

I said, "No, I want to pay you because this is how you earn your living."

He said again, "No, I do not want your money."

At this point, I noticed the man had tears in his eyes. I asked him if he would like to invite Christ to come into his life.

He then shared the following story: "I am sixty-eight years old, and I was raised in a Christian home. My mother was a woman who believed in prayer, and much of her time was spent praying for me. Mister, I have not darkened the door of a church in over fifty years. Your little boy is the first person in all those years to talk to me about Jesus. I know I need God. Will you pray for me? And thank your little boy for telling me about Jesus."

Will you allow me to ask you a personal question? How long has it been since you talked to someone about Jesus? If world evangelization is to be accomplished, each one of us must determine to be an effective witness. What is an effective witness? "One who takes the initiative to present the claims of Jesus Christ in the power of the Holy Spirit and leaves the results to God." (Dr. Bill Bright, Founder of Campus Crusade).

David was only nine years old and in the fourth grade when he shared Christ with one of his friends who then prayed to receive Christ. The world needs a lot more people like David. Will you determine to be one of them?

– 5 –

THE LORD GIVETH
AND TAKETH AWAY

~~~~~

In the early days of our ministry, we either rented a tent or a high school gymnasium, a football stadium, or whatever venue we could get. During the summer of 1989, we were scheduled for two Encounters, one in Ohio and one in Pennsylvania. We were anticipating larger crowds than our rented tent would hold, so we began to look at what it would cost to rent a larger tent.

One rental quoted us a fee of $15,000 for the week, and the other place we checked was asking $17,000 for the week. This was way beyond our budget because we had only been paying about $3,000 for the tent we had been using.

I received a call at the office one day from Sim Zook. I'd only met him a few times at Barb's home church, Conestoga Mennonite in Morgantown, Pennsylvania. This is the way the conversation went:

"Steve, I hear you need a tent." (I never found out how he had heard.)

"Yes, sir, we do. Do you know where we could find one?"

"No. But find out what one would cost and call me back."

And he hung up.

I remembered seeing an article in *Pulpit Helps* about Miami Missionary Tent Company, and I assumed they were in Miami, Florida. I looked through some old *Pulpit Helps* issues, and I found them—in Miami, Oklahoma.

I called the company and told them what I wanted. He said, "I haven't made a tent that big, but I can do it."

"Call me back and let me know what it would cost," I said.

About a week later, he called me back and said it would be $100,000.

I called Sim Zook back and told him I had found a place where we could buy a tent.

"What does it cost?"

"One hundred thousand dollars."

He said, "Order it."

I said, "I don't have $100,000."

He said, "I do. You can pay me back by renting it for a couple thousand dollars every time you use it. No interest, and I don't care how long it takes."

I took his offer to the board of our ministry, and they agreed to his terms—such as they were. There was nothing signed, just a verbal agreement.

The tent was made and purchased, and the first summer we rented it for Encounters at Berlin, Ohio, and Souderton, Pennsylvania, and I sent $6,000 to Sim Zook, $3,000 for each of the rentals.

The next year, we were doing an Encounter in Morgantown, Pennsylvania, and Mr. Zook was at the meeting every evening, Sunday night through Sunday night. On the last night, he came up to me after the service, grabbed my arm, and said, "Call me in the morning."

When I called the next morning, he said, "Tent's paid for. I don't need the money. All those people got saved last week, and that's enough for me."

So we had a $100,000 tent for $6,000.

We used that tent for a number of years, and on a hot, humid Thursday we were putting it up at the Rockingham County Fairgrounds for an Encounter we were doing the next week in my hometown of Harrisonburg, Virginia. I was in Ohio, getting ready for a crusade in Canton, Ohio, and we had a prayer rally that night. I'd left my phone back at my motel, and when I got back after the prayer rally, I saw that I had missed twenty-eight calls.

What in the world?

About six of the calls were from my son, David, so I called him first.

"What's going on?"

"Well, I've got good news and I've got bad news."

"What's the good news?"

"The tent will never hold a crowd the size we're expecting for the Encounter this week."

I had to ask, "What's the bad news?"

"We don't have a tent."

We had backed two tractor trailers lengthwise along the side of the tent. One transported the tent and the other transported the stage and choir risers. It was a large stage and the risers held a 150-voice choir. Everything had been set up and put in place, and everyone working at the setup had gone home. We were ready. A dedication service was scheduled for Saturday night, and the Encounter would start on Sunday.

The day was very hot and humid, but the temperature dropped suddenly and a recorded seventy-five-mile-per-hour wind shear came through. That straight wind hit the trailers and filled the tent like a hot air balloon—until it exploded.

Everything was totally destroyed. We found poles stuck in the ground a hundred yards away. I have one of the O-rings (which was supposed to have a 50,000-pound test on it) that held the tent strap; it was literally ripped apart. The power of that storm was just amazing.

We moved into the grandstand area at the fairgrounds, and the Encounter went on. We had a wonderful week, and God used the Encounter in a mighty way. Many people gave their lives to Christ. Just recently a gentleman saw me at a restaurant and said, "I got saved at the Encounter when you lost the tent."

My response when David told me the tent was destroyed was this: "The Lord giveth, and the Lord taketh away. Blessed be the name of the Lord."

We had insurance on the tent and we replaced it with a tent a little bit larger. God's been so good to us. I'm very, very thankful.

Several years ago, we sold the tent. It was increasingly difficult to get voluntary help to set it up at each location, and the ministry had changed because it was also increasingly difficult to get unsaved, unreached people to come to an event like an Encounter. The Encounters had become much more of a "Christian" event. I still loved doing them, but God called me to be an evangelist, so we sold the tent. The buyers used it for a relief auction in Ohio, and from there it went to Kenya. My friend there, Bishop Henry Mulandi, has invited me to come over (once we get through COVID-19) and hold an evangelistic meeting under the tent. I'm looking forward to that. I will get to preach under the tent again—in Africa! And we pray that God will allow us to see many more people come to faith in Christ.

– 6 –

OUT OF ROMANIA

Pete Lulusa

~

In 1988, God opened doors for me to go to Romania to preach the gospel. At the time, Romania was under an oppressive Communist rule, but the faith in God that I witnessed among Romanian Christians— even while they had to meet in secret—inspired my own faith. I made many lifelong friends in Romania. My good friend Pete Lulusa escaped the country many years before I first visited. This is his amazing story, in his words, of how God protected and rescued him.

We were always hungry when I was growing up in Communist Romania. After World War II, the Russian army stayed in Romania until 1958. I was eight years old when they finally left. We hated them because they took whatever they wanted from us. We would joke—because you had to have a sense of humor—and the joke was that Russia had liberated us from the Nazis, we thanked them by giving them all our corn and wheat, and then in return they also took our oil.

Romania was rich in natural resources then and is so even now. We had mountains of salt deposits, coal, gold and silver mines, copper, uranium, forests, prairies, rivers, access to the Black Sea, and the extensive and exotic wetlands of the Danube Delta. When Americans came to build orphanages in Moldova, they found three feet of black dirt. Hitler had desired our rich, black soil and had taken it out of Romania piled on freight trains.

Romania also had a great deal of oil. Many American companies like Texaco and Shell were drilling, and for twenty-five years our oil flowed constantly to Russia through a pipeline a meter in diameter until finally, as Russia's control over Romania lessened, that flow was cut off by the Romanian government.

In all the years from World War II until the revolution of 1989, one form or another of Communism controlled Romania. Under Communism, riches were taken from the rich, the rich became poorer, and the poor became richer until, at last, all were poor.

I was born in 1950, the sixth of nine children. We lived in the area of Arad, a city of economic and commercial importance, but we were very, very poor. Our family of eleven lived in a three-room house. We had no electricity and no running water. We drew drinking water from a well, and at night before going to bed, we washed in the creek running in front of the house.

We did not have beautiful clothes. Often our clothes were more patches than original material. Until I was fifteen years old, I went barefoot from March to November. In the winter, we would patch whatever shoes we had with cardboard and newspaper.

I remember being hungry all the time, and we cried because we were hungry. Sometimes we stole grapes from the vineyards. Supposedly the vineyards and farms belonged to all of us—but among "all of us," some had more rights than others.

We stood in line for everything we had to buy. We stood in line sometimes for four or five hours, and then another family member might come to take our place and stand for more hours. If there was a rumor that one store was going to have toilet paper, we would go the day before and take our place in line. There was a line for bread, another line for milk, and another for meat. You would work eight or ten hours a day, and then stand in line for the things you needed.

It was against the law to have more than a kilo (just over two pounds) of sugar in your house. If you were discovered to have more, you would be arrested.

If we were lucky, we might have meat once a month. I liked to eat meat, but there was never enough. When people asked me what I wanted to be when I grew up, I would say I wanted to be a butcher because then, I thought, there would be plenty of meat for my table. After I escaped Romania, I worked in the kitchen of a refugee camp in Italy, and when I would go to the warehouse where the food was stored I would see packages of meat with the seal that said it was Romanian beef or pork. Our president, Nicolae Ceauşescu, wanted Romania to become an industrial country, and he exported most of our meat and the best of our produce in exchange for the mighty dollars that would buy the industrial equipment.

Our family ate corn mush. Even then, we did not always have enough milk for the mush. I often left school early to take the cow to pasture in the hills. We had nothing else to feed her, but we needed her milk.

My family was not always so poor. My father was a blacksmith. Before Communism, our town had six thousand people owning four hundred eighty pair of oxen and one thousand horses. Five black-smiths in town were always busy, and my father was well-to-do. All of that disappeared, though, and from the time of my earliest memories, we were one of the poorest families in town.

We did not suffer poverty only because of the government's economic policies; we were also poor because our family was Christian and not members of the Communist Party. Christians were harassed and oppressed.

We were mistreated in every way possible. For example, we would go to the forest to pick up branches for our fires. We'd carry home the bundles of wood on our backs, but sometimes those in charge of the forest would stop us and make us leave the bundles behind. They would rather the wood rot in the forest than we have the comfort of its warmth. I remember that we chopped up our wood fence to keep warm and cook.

On Sunday morning from nine o'clock to one o'clock we went to school. There we were shown a movie meant to indoctrinate us against capitalism and the West. If we were not at the movie, we were ridiculed, punished, and mocked.

In an attempt to control the people, the government had an elaborate network of informants. Everyone was spying on everyone else. Parents informed against children, brother against brother, grandchildren against grandparents, and church member against pastors. Even one of the leaders in our church was an official in the Communist Party.

Every Monday, pastors had to go and give declaration of what they had preached on Sunday. Their reports would be compared to the reports of the spies in the church. No pastor could preach about the kingdom of God or anything that stood against the government.

The spies in the church danced to Communist music and always seemed to have everything they needed. We would say about them, "They eat whiter bread than the rest of us."

I felt like the whole world was against us. I am a very free spirit, and I asked *why*; I wanted to know the reasons for our poverty and persecution. I wanted to know why we could not travel freely. As I grew, I became a troublemaker with an angry spirit. My mother was Pentecostal and my father Baptist, so I grew up in a Christian home and I knew what it meant to belong to God. But when I was sixteen, I ran away from the church and from God.

One thing that Communism did for people was to give them an education and a trade. At sixteen, I went to trade school in Arad and learned foundry work. When I graduated in 1968, I got a job in a factory, doing work with bronze, cast iron, and aluminum.

Finally, I had money to buy clothes. I had money for wine too. We lived in a country where wine was plentiful, and we had more wine than milk. I don't like to dwell on the sins of my past, but I used to get very crazy with my friends. (We all like to blame our friends for our faults!)

My voice was good enough that I sang in nightclubs. There I would receive free drinks from managers and customers. I was often in fights. My head was busted a few times with beer bottles or chairs. Sometimes I was arrested or fined. I was always in trouble with the law. My mother would say, "When you leave home on Saturday evening to go out, you look like an executive. When you come home, you look like a pig."

I caused a lot of shame to God, my parents, and my church. I had already been put out of church because I loved to dance, and I had been seen dancing at a wedding.

So neither the church nor the world wanted me. The world rejected me because I came from a Christian family and was not a member of the Communist Party. I was a second-class citizen. The church rejected me because I could not follow its legalistic standards. I saw no future for myself in Romania. There had to be something better.

My eyes were first opened to life outside Romania when a family friend from Vancouver, British Columbia, visited us. I asked him about life in America. He said there were no problems crossing the border from Canada to the United States and everyone traveled without restrictions. In America, you were allowed to take the job of your choice and you could buy a car. I was seventeen, and I began to think about running away and going to America.

By the time I had finished trade school and had a job, I was really serious about finding a way to leave Romania. I knew the only way to get out of Romania was to go to Yugoslavia as a tourist for one day and make my escape from there. A number of us had permission to go to the city of Belgrade on a group passport. Besides going as tourists, we took knickknacks to sell to people on the street. I was permitted to go as part of the group because my uncle put in a good word for me.

Only two people knew of my plan to escape. I had told my youngest brother, Paul. He was a Christian and was walking with God. A few weeks after I told him of my plan, he came to me and said, "Pete, I prayed for you, and you're gonna make it."

I had no idea how I was going to make it out of Romania, but I prayed too. Even though I had no power to stay on course as a Christian, I tried to bargain with God. I told Him, "If You help me get to America, I will give You my heart."

The other person who knew of my desire to escape was my best friend, Peter. We grew up together, and we talked about leaving Romania together. We planned to hide on the train, the Oriental Express that came from Turkey through Belgrade and ran all the way to Paris. Once out of Yugoslavia, we would find our way to Italy or Austria and then to America.

Peter also went with the tour group, and we boarded the bus to Belgrade on August 24, 1969, a rainy day.

But once we were in Yugoslavia, Peter was afraid. He thought we would be caught. People caught at checkpoints were sent back to Romania and automatically sentenced to anywhere from three to five years imprisonment. And when you're running, a tremendous fear overtakes you. You feel everyone knows you are guilty. In addition, Peter had dreams of joining the Securitate, the secret police. He was my friend, but he could not take a chance on America. A job in the Securitate would give him a few more privileges than most Romanians.

We actually flipped a coin to decide if we would go back to Romania or try to get to America. We flipped the coin three times because I was determined to leave and Peter wanted to go back. In the end, we said goodbye. He went home, and I was alone.

In Belgrade, I ate some bread and salami on a park bench. I would need a ticket to get on the train, but I could not speak the language and had no idea how I would buy my ticket. I asked a man to take me to the train station, but he had to go to work. He taught me words to ask for a ticket, and I practiced them over and over, maybe a million times.

But when I stood in front of a ticket window, I could not remember the words. The woman at the window grew angry with me and called me crazy and a devil, and so I left her window because I was afraid to make a commotion. There were a lot of police in the station, and I did not want to draw attention.

I looked for someone who would buy the ticket for me, someone with a kind face that would not turn me in. A younger man understood my words, "Romania, fugitive, Italia," and took my money and bought my ticket to Trieste, the last checkpoint at the border between Yugoslavia and Italy.

I had a ticket but no passport. I would need another kind person to help me, someone who would sit with me on the train as though we were traveling together. I approached a young lady with the same words, "Romania. Fugitive. Italia." She understood that I wanted her to take me with her onto the train and she held my ticket and took me to her compartment. She offered me food, and after we had eaten, I went to sleep.

I was awakened when the conductor came into the compartment, checking tickets. On the international trains, there are always police with the conductor. But for some reason, the policeman decided to smoke a cigarette in the corridor and he did not come in.

The lady gave the conductor our tickets, both hers and mine. She pretended that I was deaf and mute. The conductor said my ticket was not in order. I had a ticket for the train, but I did not have a seat ticket, with the car number and the compartment number. I would have to pay more money, he said. I paid him and he left. The policeman never came in.

I fell asleep again. The lady woke me up as the train neared Zagreb. I saw her ahead of me, getting off the train, and then she vanished and I never saw her again.

Sooner or later, all passengers would have to show proper traveling papers, and I did not have them. The train would go on to Ljubljana, but I knew I had to be off the train before I was questioned about papers.

I got off the train about midnight and started back along the cars. The first car back was a sleeping car, and I knew I was not supposed to be there. Those doors were all closed, so that was not even a possibility. Someone hollered. I did not know if anyone was watching me, but when I came to another car that had both doors open—on both sides—I jumped through the car. I saw one man leaning out a window, watching me. I kept walking down the other side of the train.

Down the line, I crawled under a car and looked for places to hang onto the chassis and to position myself. As soon as I got under the train, before I could find the right spot, I saw a flashlight approaching and heard the sound of the train wheels being struck with a hammer. Someone was checking for cracks in the wheels. An unusual sound would mean there was a crack. My thigh was resting on the axle, and I knew this would change the sound when the hammer struck, and I would be discovered.

I lifted myself off the axle. The light flashed fully on my face but the hammer went by.

I had to move. I could not stay on the axle; it began turning as soon as the train moved. Rolling to the outside of the train, I swung my body up to get on top of the chassis.

Dust and stones flew up at me as the train rolled along. Even worse, I had chosen a spot close to the outlet for the car's sanitary equipment. For hours I rode with filth of all kinds spraying over me, and by the time daylight had come, I was covered with oil, dust, dirt, and sewage. But I kept praying and rejoicing and praising God for where I was.

At seven in the morning, the train came to a stop at the Yugoslavian checkpoint before Trieste, Italy. We stayed there for two hours. Soldiers with assault rifles and leashed guard dogs walked up and down the platform. I could see the dogs; I could have reached out and touched them, but they did not detect me. With my covering of filth, I may not have smelled like a human.

No one saw me. Three men came along, checking the wheels, and one bent over and looked straight into my eyes. I really believe that I did make eye contact with him. But no one said a word, and they moved on. God, who made the eye, can also close the eyes. And perhaps He closed those eyes that day.

The next stop was Trieste. I had wanted to go to Paris, but by this time I was very, very tired. The train stopped at Trieste for almost an hour, and I debated with myself. Should I get out? Should I stay hidden? I was hearing a lot of people speaking Italian, but was I safe?

Finally, I crawled out of my hiding place. I must have been quite a sight, bedraggled, filthy, and smelly. But I asked the first man I met, "Italia?"

"*Sì*," he answered.

I threw my bag in the air and rejoiced. People were watching, and they cheered and applauded the refugee. I asked for political asylum and it was granted.

In Italy, I stayed in a refugee camp. The camp was created from the remains of a Nazi concentration camp, and we slept in barracks the Germans had built for prisoners.

After I had been in the camp eight months, the pastor of a Romanian Baptist Church in Detroit became my sponsor, and I came to America on April 28, 1970. I did not forget the deal I had made with God, and two months later I gave my heart to Christ and my new life began.

I thank God for my new life and that I am here. And sometimes I still don't believe it. But I do believe God had a plan for me since the day I was born. That was why He brought me out of Romania.

I have not forgotten the incredible poverty and the terrible hunger. Now I count myself among the richest and most privileged people in the world. God has given me a new life and blessed me and spoiled me—and I am not speaking of finances.

– 7 – •

IN THE DARKNESS, FIRE OF REVIVAL

~

Almost nineteen years after Pete Lulusa had found a home in the United States, I (Steve) was on a road in Hungary, driving toward the border of Romania, the safety of my own homeland left behind. As we drove toward the outer boundaries of the tightly guarded Communist domain, a heavy, oppressive sense of darkness closed around our car. We could see the power of that darkness on people's faces and in their body language, and even in the bleakness of the landscapes through which we passed.

Although the Romanian dictator Nicolae Ceaușescu showed a friendly, progressive face to the outside world, the impenetrable Iron Curtain had dropped around that country, cutting off the Romanian people from the outside world and even from other Communist neighbors. We had heard rumors and firsthand stories, like Pete Lulusa's, about the suffering in Romania, but travel into and out of the country was tightly regulated, and Romania's communication with the outside world was limited to whatever the government-controlled media wanted the world to hear.

On that day in December of 1988, Mike was the only one in the car who had been in Romania before—and thus he was the only one who knew firsthand what we were driving into. A few miles from the border crossing, he began shaking with apprehension. The darkness of what lay ahead so unsettled him that he felt sick and was soon hyperventilating. We stopped to buy him crackers and a Coke, and he walked around the car several times, trying to calm down. The Coke he sipped would be the last one we'd see for three weeks.

Crossing the border into Hungary had been intimidating enough as we were subjected to probing questions and searches. Now we were within minutes of leaving Hungary and entering Communist Romania, and whatever Mike knew that the rest of us did not know was pushing him to a state of near panic.

The cold wind swirled snow across the road, and a dark foreboding pressed into us as we crossed a stretch of no man's land and approached the chain link fences, guard towers, and soldiers holding machine guns. As we drove through one opening, the heavy gate dropped behind us. We were in Romania; there was no going back. We weren't going forward, either; ahead, more guards and guns and yet another gate blocked our progress.

The first question from the soldier was, "Do you have a Bible?" Although I was going to preach, I had followed advice to leave my own Bible at the hotel in Vienna and borrow one when I got into Romania.

"No," I said.

"Do you have any pornography?"

"No."

"Do you have drugs?"

"No."

"Arms and ammunition?"

"No."

For the first time in my life, I was traveling behind the Iron Curtain. The Berlin Wall still slashed that city in two and cut down anyone who tried to cross the boundary; all along the western borders of the Communist Bloc, guns and roadblocks denied freedom of travel. Were I and my three friends crazy, trying to pull back that grim curtain and go into the darkness behind it? Perhaps, in the eyes of the world. There was certainly a great danger; we were probably risking our lives, and at the least, our freedom. Yet we know that the Lord uses what the world calls foolish to accomplish His purposes. We were obeying Him and, as my friend Ike Stoltzfus has said, we were planting our tiny mustard seed of faith.

This border crossing was the same place at which my friend Sammy Tippit had been ushered out of Communist Romania. Sammy is a Southern Baptist evangelist; he had been boldly preaching the gospel in Romania while Nicolae Ceaușescu claimed to be building a utopia. In reality, Ceaușescu was persecuting not only the church but all of the Romanian people. My friend Sammy was arrested, taken to the country's border, and told he could never again enter Romania or preach there.

Sammy could not go back to Romania, but he had already scheduled preaching engagements for December of 1988 and January of 1989. Knowing that any communication from him might endanger the Romanian churches he had promised to visit, he did not cancel his events. Instead, he asked me to go and preach in his place.

I immediately felt that the Lord wanted me to go to Romania, and I agreed to go and preach.

Two friends traveled with me, board members of Wingfield Ministries, Ike Stoltzfus from Pennsylvania and Bill Overstreet from Virginia. Sammy arranged a contact to travel with us; we had flown into Vienna, Austria, and had met Mike there. Driving a rented vehicle, we first entered Hungary, also a Communist-controlled country, and drove to Budapest, where we spent the night.

Now I was staring at the Romanian border guards, at their guns and grim faces. After the questions, they searched our luggage and inspected the car, tapping on the sides and pulling it over a pit (similar to an oil-changing pit) to check the underside with mirrors. They ordered us to hand over our passports for scrutiny, separated us, and questioned us individually. We endured body searches.

Finally, four hours later, the gate went up and we were allowed to proceed.

We checked into our rooms at Băile Felix, a health resort built around some of Romania's many hot springs, and in the evening drove into the nearby city of Oradea to meet our contact who would take us to our first speaking engagement.

Again, we had been strongly warned to follow precautions: park a half mile away from the apartment complex where our contact lived, do not speak after we get out of the car. People lived in fear of the Securitate, the secret police. It was said that Ceaușescu had eleven thousand agents and half a million informers. In any group of four people, chances were good that at least one of them was an informer, and you never knew whether what you said would soon be reported to Securitate officials. Even the churches were infiltrated with informers. As they went about their daily lives, Romanians never knew who was watching, who was listening, and who might be the next person arrested and taken away—sometimes to disappear forever. Fear lived in every corner of the country.

We walked in silence through the bitterly cold, dark evening, with the snow still falling around us. The city was dark and quiet. Tram cars were forced to run without lights at night. The new snow could not hide the ugliness and the sadness of what Ceaușescu had done to this city.

One of the dictator's programs had confiscated farms, leveled villages, and forced people to move into the cities, where the government built huge concrete apartment buildings to house many people in tiny spaces. The government controlled as much of life as it could: where you lived, how you lived, what you ate, what you believed, where you traveled, what you said, and who could or could not visit you.

Conditions were deplorable. Ceaușescu had boasted that under his Communist rule there would be no mud in Romania. If you ever have the privilege of visiting Romania, you'll see that in spring and summer there's mud, mud, and more mud everywhere. But Ceaușescu promised that Communism would meet every need and create a perfect environment, even to the point of eliminating the mud. The mud is still in Romania, and the utopia Ceaușescu had proclaimed turned out to be a sentence of torture and misery for the people of this country.

Ceaușescu's government became one of the most restrictive of all the Communist countries. Prior to World War II, Romania was a wealthy country, often referred to as the breadbasket of Europe. At one time, Bucharest was known as the Paris of the Balkans and Timișoara was the City of Flowers. Yet under Ceaușescu's reign, all of that was lost. The Romanians now lived in extreme fear and want.

I learned much on that first visit behind the Iron Curtain. If you lived in Romania in 1988, you stood in food lines for hours. You'd stand in one line to buy milk, then another line to buy eggs. You waited for hours, and sometimes you hired someone else to stand in line for you. When meat was available, you'd get in line, and if you finally reached the front of the line, an axe hacked off a chunk and you'd take whatever cut you were given. As in so much of life in this oppressed country, you would have no choices.

The snow kept coming down as we trudged through drab and dreary streets that night, and I thought how sad it was to see what Ceaușescu's greed and tyranny had done to this country. Far from the promised utopia, the once flourishing, wealthy Romania was now a prisoner of unbelievable poverty, drained of energy and vigor by a regime of cruelty and repression. And while the general population lived on so little, the dictator was selling Romania's resources to other countries to fund the building of a palace for his own residence and his government functions. The palace was so grand that it was the world's second largest building, lavish in its use of gold, marble, and crystal. Ceaușescu called it the People's House, but in reality, the people of Romania were stripped of their wealth to pay for his extravagant and luxurious lifestyle. The construction of the monstrous building was also an excuse for the government to raze many beautiful old buildings and destroy churches and temples in Bucharest.

There were no words between us as we walked in the dark, cold night, but when we approached two gray apartment buildings, I noticed Mike's hesitation and indecision. He had only been here once before, and now it was obvious he did not remember which building was the correct one. "Lord, direct him to the right one," I prayed.

Mike turned to the building on the right.

We entered a dark hallway; there were no lights, and we used flashlights to find our way up four flights of stairs. Even inside the building, it was bitterly cold. Heat and electricity were rationed by the government. Those utilities would be available for only a few hours each day.

When we knocked on an apartment door, an elderly lady answered, and I could tell immediately that Mike did not know her and she did not recognize him. Had he, after all, chosen the wrong place?

"*Pace, pace,*" Mike said. It is the Christian greeting in Romania. It means *peace.*

"*Pace,*" replied the lady. She could not speak English, but she was apparently expecting us. She ushered us into the apartment. "Moment, Titus. Moment, Titus." Titus Coltea was the man we had come to meet, and we took her words to mean that he would be there shortly.

We sat down to wait, talking with each other. The apartment consisted of a tiny kitchen, a small living room, a bathroom, and one bedroom. The lady who had greeted us was Titus's mother-in-law; she was taking care of the children. Soon Titus, a medical doctor about thirty-five years old, and his wife came in and were elated to see us.

"Praise God! I knew you would be here. God told me you would be here, and I've arranged for you to preach at our church tonight."

Even though I had changed into a coat and tie, expecting to speak, I felt some surprise at this. After all, it was Friday night and the snow was still coming down heavily. I'm from Virginia—back home, this weather would have been cause to call off any scheduled event. Titus's excitement, though, would not be canceled by cold or snow.

The Colteas served us tea, a piece of bread, and an eggplant dip often served in Romania, and then we left for the church. The streets were nearly empty, and I could not help but think, *It's snowing like crazy. Who would come out on a night like this? Why are we doing this?*

Through what seemed to be a back door, we entered a large building that looked like a warehouse. One of the church's deacons met us in an office that was almost as raw and cold as the weather outside. We gathered around a coal stove and tried to warm our shivering bodies. A few minutes later, several more men arrived. Everyone seemed very excited, although of course I couldn't understand everything that was said. We had prayer, and then I was told to follow the men to the pulpit. *Well, evidently they expect at least a few people to be here.*

I followed them through a door, totally unprepared for what I was about to experience.

More than two thousand people had crowded into the building. We pushed our way through the mass of bodies to the pulpit, and from that vantage point, I could see that there was standing room only. People stood along the walls and filled the aisles and the foyer. Sometimes a person who did have a seat stood and offered their place to another. I learned later that it was often Christians who gave up their seats to the unsaved.

For the first hour, they prayed. As the snow and cold swirled outside, the presence of God, real and powerful, filled that place. I wept at the intensity of the prayers and thought, *What do I have to say to these people?*

Then the song service began. A full orchestra accompanied a choir of hundreds of voices. I watched and listened, sitting there in total amazement. These people had lived under persecution for decades.

Twenty years before, Ceaușescu had set out to eliminate the church in Romania. Communism would supply every need, he claimed; there would be no need for God and the church. Congregations were permitted to meet as long as the meetings were inside a building. But that night at the Second Baptist Church in Oradea, I was a witness to the exciting things the Lord was doing—in spite of the government's attempt to erase God from Romanian minds and hearts.

As the service went on, the pastor leaned over with an apology. Since it was Friday night, he said, many of his people had to work and could not attend. But there were probably five hundred more people outside, listening over the speaker system. This church was the largest Baptist church in all of Europe; the largest Pentecostal church in Europe was also in Romania. Ceaușescu could not banish God from this country.

Titus translated for me as I preached, and God moved in a powerful way. Hundreds of people were saved. I will never forget that first wonderful, wonderful evening with Romanian Christians.

Following the service, we were invited to the senior pastor's home, and Pastor Nick began to tell us stories of persecution in Romania. It was a reign of terror for all Romanians, but Christians especially were persecuted. Even our fellowship at the pastor's home was forbidden. Romanians could not welcome Westerners in their homes, and even socializing with each other was restricted.

While Ceaușescu's Communist regime was busy trying to eliminate God from Romania, God was moving, using the persecution to grow His church.

The Second Baptist Church in Oradea, where I had just preached to thousands, had started as a Bible study led by Titus Coltea's father. The house church flourished as God moved in the city, and Dr. Coltea felt called by God to give up his law practice and pastor the congregation.

The exponential growth of his church drew the disapproval and opposition of the Communist authorities. Dr. Coltea was arrested, pronounced "crazy," and committed to a mental institution. After some time there, he was moved to a prison and then given a job intended to intimidate and humiliate him: his job would be to clean the city sewers.

At that time in Romania, very few had freedom of travel, even within the country. Anyone who wanted to go from one city to another first had to go to city hall and apply for a visa to visit another city. No one dared travel without first reporting to the authorities and obtaining permission.

But as a sewer cleaner, Dr. Coltea traveled all over Romania. Of course, he traveled under guard, but nevertheless he had opportunity to move about the country. Down into the sewers he went, killing rats and working at a job no one would willingly take on. His persecutors taunted him, told him he was crazy, and urged him to deny Christ. Instead, Dr. Coltea shared his faith in every city above the sewers he cleaned. Revival spread all over Romania as God worked in persecution meant for evil and used it to grow the church. I love the way God does things!

Pastor Nick told us the church was still being watched and persecuted. I had already noticed that inside the church walls, Romanians were alive and excited as they sang and prayed. But as soon as they walked out, they grew quiet, speaking only in whispers. They never knew who was listening and who might report to the authorities anything that was said. Even in their homes they lived in fear; a radio or television was usually turned on, in hopes that conversations could not be miked or recorded. About two weeks before we arrived, the authorities had called in Nick and his wife and played a cassette tape of a conversation they had had in the privacy of their own bedroom. The threat was clear: the authorities were watching, and anyone who spoke the wrong thing would suffer consequences.

I'm convinced the authorities did not have the technology to monitor everyone. They didn't need to—all they needed to do was make an example of a few people. Intimidation, cruelty, and censorship had been effective, and the entire country was gripped by the fear of being watched, taped, or reported.

The next morning, we scraped snow and ice from the car before we could set out on snow-covered roads. Cars shared the road with horse-drawn carts and, at one place, we crept along behind a flock of sheep that stubbornly refused to turn aside or move off the roadway. Our route took us through small villages where many stores and shops were boarded up and deserted. It was a bleak landscape in every way, even though Ceaușescu had posted his propaganda signs everywhere, proclaiming his regime of hope.

I preached for three weeks on that first trip to Romania in the last days of 1988 and the first weeks of 1989. Many times, the church would be full, with people standing in the aisles, in corners, and in the balconies. Church buildings often looked tired and beaten, with patched ceilings and walls. The extreme poverty in the country had stripped away so much in the lives of the Romanians. Worn faces looked up at me, looking for hope—faces etched with deep lines, faces showing the heavy burdens these people bore.

Still, worship with these brothers and sisters in Christ was sweet. The people were generous and warm-hearted, sharing what little they had. One Sunday morning communion service was especially moving, as we felt the unity of the Spirit of Christ and a warm, deep love not often experienced in the United States. We understood none of the words of hymns, but we recognized the music—songs like "Sweet Hour of Prayer." Ike Stoltzfus observed that at times it seemed the choir music was piped in directly from heaven.

From Oradea we went to Cluj, Brăila, and Alba Iulia, and we ended with a series of meetings at the First Baptist Church in Timișoara, where Peter Dugalescu was the pastor.

Peter had been the pastor of a church in the small town of Orăştie when God called him to the university town of Timişoara. Obeying, Peter moved to the much larger city, but he made the move without the mandatory permission from the government. Even when given direct orders to leave Timişoara, he stayed, determined to obey God.

When the authorities realized intimidation would not move him, persecution intensified and attempts were made on his life. One day he found himself trapped on a one-way street with a bus barreling down on him. The bus broadsided his car, and Peter was taken to the hospital with injuries that included a broken arm. While he was in surgery, a doctor removed his oxygen supply. But one of the nurses in the operating room was a Christian, and when she saw what the doctor had done, she began praying. We believe God breathed into Peter's lungs that day and spared his life. He survived, recovered, and continued to pastor First Baptist Church.

Years later, one of the secret police who came to Christ told us he had once had Peter in the sights of his long-range rifle. He pulled the trigger, but it did not fire. He squeezed again and again, but the gun did not go off. Finally, he pulled his firearm back, wondering what was wrong, and once the gun moved away from his target, it fired. How many times God miraculously saved Peter's life, we will not know this side of heaven.

We began a series of nightly meetings at First Baptist and a revival broke out in Timişoara. I preached in two services each evening. At every service, people filled up the church and more stood outside in the courtyard, standing in the cold to hear God's Word. Then the Third Baptist Church invited me to preach, and I agreed to be at their service after the two at First Baptist. So I was preaching at seven o'clock, eight o'clock, and nine o'clock. The Fifth Baptist Church called and we scheduled a service there at five o'clock. The presence of God was felt all over the city and hundreds of people came to Christ.

Even while trying to stamp out Christianity, Ceauşescu's Communist regime did allow some churches to meet if they were authorized by the government. The other churches I had preached in were authorized, but the Fifth Baptist Church was not. So there I was, preaching in an unauthorized, illegal church. And it wasn't long before Peter Dugalescu and I were standing in the headquarters of the Timişoara secret police.

The conversation was in Romanian, so Peter spoke for us both. The Romanian language is Latin-based and conveys a lot of emotional overtones, and this conversation was particularly animated. I knew they were talking about me.

"Peter, what's he saying?" I asked.

Peter pounded the desk with his fist. "He said you cannot preach anymore."

"And what did you tell him?"

Peter's fist hit the desk again. "I said, 'We're going to obey God!'"

Obeying God meant openly defying the Communist authority. I'll be honest—I felt some trepidation. I didn't want to go to jail. I wanted to be able to go home to my country where I could travel and preach with no restraints. Would I, instead, end up in a cell somewhere, completely cut off from my family and friends back home, detained for as long as the government pleased?

Then I thought about the man representing me in the face of this threat. Peter had stood here before. Every time the secret police tried to control what he was doing or preaching, he had to decide where to place his loyalty. We make that choice daily in America, too, but here in Romania, Christians were laying their lives on the line when they chose to be obedient to God.

We were given a stern warning and were free to leave. I left there certain that no matter the cost, my choice must always be to obey my God.

Nothing Ceaușescu and his Securitate could do would have stopped the revival that spread through Timișoara. I preached from one Sunday to the next, and at every meeting, God moved in a powerful way.

As I stood in the pulpit the final Sunday, I promised to return to Romania by the end of that year. I also promised to return with an invitation for Peter to come to the National Prayer Breakfast with the President of the United States. Peter almost fainted in his surprise.

"You're kidding," he said.

"No, I'm going to come back with an invitation for you from the President of the United States."

I knew the secret police were watching every move Peter made, and I knew threats had been made against him. But I wanted to send a message—if there was an informer in the service that day (and there was a good chance there was at least one), then I hoped if Ceaușescu's government understood that the international community was watching what was going on in Romania and Peter Dugalescu was known in the outside world, the persecution might let up.

Returning to the States in January of 1989, I began making plans for my return to Romania, which would again be in the last week of the year. In October, Ed Scearce, a staff member and partner in ministry, went to Romania to do some preparation work for my trip and decide which cities I'd visit. Ike Stoltzfus was also on that planning trip, and he came home and reported that conditions in Romania were even worse than what we had seen on our first trip. He wrote:

> Returning on my second trip in October of 1989 with Steve's ministry, we found conditions in Romania had worsened, becoming even darker with Ceaușescu's tightening grip of oppression while countries around them were opening up to the West. Food shortages—gas lines—bread lines worsened. Church leaders Paul, Peter, and Titus, encouraged us to share in America what they were experiencing. I will never forget

the night we were driving home from a church service. We drove by a "roadkill" rabbit lying in the road. The church leader asked us to turn around to pick it up. That's how desperate things had become.

I knew I would definitely be going back to Timișoara; I had already secured the invitation for Peter to come to the National Prayer Breakfast in the States. We also made arrangements for Titus Coltea and his wife, Gabi, to come. Gabi had a severe skin disorder and would be treated at the University of Virginia. In December, we would go back to Romania with those invitations in hand.

By the fall of 1989, dissatisfaction with Communist rule finally erupted into civil protests and anti-government demonstrations throughout Communist countries in Eastern Europe. We in America watched our television screens as the Iron Curtain began to open, and less than a month after my team had been in Romania, East Germany's borders were declared open and the Berlin Wall—the most infamous symbol of the Iron Curtain—began to be dismantled. We saw the images of celebrating people dancing on the wall. In many countries, the Communist governments began crumbling under the pressure of numerous and large demonstrations, most of them peaceful with little bloodshed.

But in Romania, Ceaușescu stubbornly tightened his hold, and so the revolution, when it came to that country, was violent and bloody.

It all began in the city I was so eager to revisit and where I now claimed dear friends—in the city of Timișoara.

– 8 –

"GOD EXISTS!".

~

László Tőkés was a popular pastor in the city of Timişoara, and his Reformed church was growing rapidly. In addition, Tőkés had spoken openly against Ceauşescu, the dictator's brutal policies, and the Communist Party. By December of 1989, the authorities, alarmed by the pastor's growing influence, decided to take steps to quiet him. Tőkés was notified he would be evicted from his home and banished from the city.

On Friday, December 15, authorities arrived at the pastor's home to "escort" him out of town. They were met by a human barricade surrounding the house and the church to which it was attached. Several hundred Baptist and Pentecostal youths stood between the police and the pastor and his family. The group had no weapons but sang hymns and stood their ground to prevent the police from taking Tőkés. Daniel, a young man from First Baptist Church, had brought candles; he distributed them among the youth, and the flames lit the December night, representing Christ, the Light of the world.

As sympathetic passersby learned what was happening, they joined in the protest to protect the pastor and his family. The police turned fire hoses on them, attempting to break down their resistance, but still the assembly grew. The protest at the church was peaceful, but the anger, frustration, and dissatisfaction simmering in the city was beginning to boil, and during the night some fights between protesters and police broke out in other streets throughout the city. On

Saturday, Securitate forces and the army were brought in to crush the citywide protests. Demonstrators were beaten or arrested. While skirmishes spilled through the streets and spread across Timişoara, the standoff at the church continued.

Early Sunday morning, one of my Romanian friends, Eugen, awoke early and walked through the city center. He remembers feeling a great weight on his heart. The heaviness in the air was a physical thing, a feeling he said he had never felt before and has not felt since. He wondered if something were physically wrong with him. Now he looks back and wonders if what he felt was the oppression of the powers of darkness and evil gathering in that city, because that Sunday would bring a terrible bloodbath in Timişoara.

That day, the police finally broke through the resistance at László Tőkés's church. They beat the pastor and took him away to an isolated mountain village. By now the crowd was huge, and thousands of people began marching toward the Communist headquarters in the city center. The weekend had begun with hymns and prayers, a peaceful resistance to Tőkés's removal. But the authorities' heavy-handed actions against demonstrators simply stoked the hot, smoldering embers of anger and revolt burning throughout the city.

Army tanks moved in. The crowds would not disperse. Soldiers used bayonets on the people for the first time, and then they were given orders to start shooting. It was a terrible scene, as Ceauşescu's government started slaughtering its own people, including young people and children.

At one point, an ambulance pulled up in front of the cathedral. Wounded people rushed toward it, but when its doors opened, it was filled with more soldiers inside who fired machine guns on the crowd. Some tried to run to the cathedral for refuge, but the doors had been locked, and they were mowed down right there on the cathedral steps.

Eugen tells me he saw terrible things that day, things he will never forget. Many people died. Some "disappeared," never to be seen again. In some cases, families never found their loved ones' bodies.

The young man Daniel was in the crowd again; again, he had distributed and lit candles. His fiancée was holding his right arm as they marched, and he felt her fall to the ground beside him as the shooting began. Then pain burned through his right leg. His fiancée died, and Daniel lost his leg. Later, when I visited him, he would tell me, "Steve, it's OK. I lit the first candle!"

Hundreds of people died that Sunday night in Timişoara. And still the crowds did not go home. An inferno of revolution was raging through the city and would not be snuffed out. Eugen remembers that it began to rain in the early hours of Monday morning, but the people, subjugated for so long, now refused to bow to the government's powers. By Monday morning, the streets of Timişoara were covered with broken glass and scattered pieces of bloody clothing. The city was almost shut down—workers were on strike, shops and businesses were closed, and a tidal wave of humanity, unstoppable, still swirled toward the city center.

Over the next few days, the demonstrations became a groundswell of the oppressed rising in revolt against the oppressor. Defying curfews and the threat of the army, people poured into the streets saying, "We have nothing else to live for." They marched and sang patriotic songs that had been banned for decades.

Ceauşescu attempted to seal off Timişoara, trying to keep news of the revolt from spreading to the rest of the country. Later, it was rumored that he had also ordered the bombing of all of Timişoara. If that rumor is true, then it was only the mercy of God that blocked the execution of that order.

The demonstrators would not go home or silence their voices. Eugen and other Christians stayed in the city center. Sometimes they sang Christian songs; sometimes they knelt in the streets and prayed the Lord's Prayer. Often the chant went up, "God exists! God exists! God exists!"

The fire was ignited. The government tried to stamp out the flames that had been set ablaze by what Ceaușescu called the "rabble" in Timișoara. But the revolt could not be contained, and news of what was happening in Timișoara drifted across the country, carrying the sparks that lit violence in other cities, including the capital, Bucharest.

Ceaușescu announced a huge rally in support of the government. He had staged many such speeches before, to impress and manipulate the crowds.

This time, his plan failed. Half a million people flooded the square in front of the Central Committee Building in Bucharest, from which he normally made his speeches. But this crowd would not be impressed, manipulated, or appeased. Ceaușescu's address was shouted down by anti-government slogans, outright booing, and chants of "Timișoara! Timișoara!" The demonstrators burned posters and pictures of the dictator. Ceaușescu was forced to retreat into the building.

Like a volcano, Bucharest was erupting. The army soon saw that there was no holding back this revolution, and many soldiers began to take the side of the people, put down their weapons, and refused to fire on the protestors.

The story has been widely reported that Ceaușescu told the National Minister of Defense, General Vasile Milea, to give the order to the army to fire on the crowds. When the general refused, he was accused of treason. The next day, while talking to his wife on the phone, he was killed by a gunshot. Although General Milea's family was told that the general took his own life, most people believe he was killed for resisting Ceaușescu's orders.

Ceaușescu tried one more time to talk to the crowds. He was met with burning rage. The mob tried to attack the building. Scattered gunfire provoked panic. In the ensuing chaos, Ceaușescu gave up on his speech, and he and his wife fled from the city in a helicopter.

In Timişoara, two hundred thousand demonstrators had gathered in the city square. Here, too, the army had changed sides and no longer fought against the demonstrators. From the balcony of the opera house, leaders of the revolution encouraged the people to stand strong and not be afraid—*We are going to win!* they declared. But when the demand came to hear from a pastor, no church leader dared to speak.

My friend Peter Dugalescu was there.

"I must speak," he said. His family tried to dissuade him. The crowd was still disorderly and unpredictable. Gunfire might come at any time, from any direction. But Peter insisted, "I must go and speak."

From the balcony of the opera house, Peter began his message by talking about their lives under Communism. The government had torn down churches and persecuted believers and tried to convince the people that there was no God and they had no need of God. "But," said Peter, "I want to talk to you in the name of this God."

As he spoke, someone slipped him a note. He glanced down, read it, and I can only imagine the feelings that must have flooded through him. Interrupting his message, he gave the news to the crowd: "We have just received word that Ceauşescu has fled from the palace."

The shouts started and spread across the square.

"God exists! God exists! God is with us!"

For nearly a generation, Nicolae Ceauşescu had tried to make God unnecessary, to prove, even, that there was no God. But now that shout of *Immanuel! God is with us!* rang throughout all of Romania at Christmas of 1989. Just as Jesus was born one night almost two thousand years before so that He could bring hope to a dark world, so He came to bring hope to Romania at Christmastime in one of the darkest periods of her history.

Peter finally quieted the crowd and said, "At this historic moment, we need to pray." Just days before, people had been gunned down for kneeling in the streets and praying for their city. But now as Peter began the Lord's Prayer, two hundred thousand people knelt on the streets of Timişoara and joined in, voicing a prayer to the God who has always existed. Peter told me it sounded like the voices of angels echoing off the walls of the centuries-old buildings.

"It was not a revolution, it was a miracle," Peter told me later. "They had guns, they had tanks, they had an army. All we had were songs and prayers and candles. And we won."

Eugen, too, talks of the miracles God performed that week in Romania. God orchestrated His purposes even within the evil events of those days. For one thing, that December was the warmest December in Romania for over a century. Romanian winters are bitterly cold. In any other December, it would have been far too cold for the crowds to be outdoors for those long days and nights.

Ceauşescu himself, when he called for the rally, brought together the mass of people who would rise up against him and demand an end to his rule. With the populace under the strict and suspicious surveillance of the Securitate, revolutionaries could never have organized such a large demonstration. People were too afraid to talk to each other about their dissatisfaction or their plans. You never knew if you might be talking to an informant. Yet, Ceauşescu's plan (which I'm inclined to think was really God's plan) to stage a rally brought half a million people to Bucharest. Only God's hand could make such a thing possible.

On Christmas Day, Ceauşescu and his wife were captured and executed "for crimes and atrocities" against the Romanian people. Twenty years before, the tyrant had promised a utopia with no mud and no need for God. Romania still has plenty of mud. And God did amazing things in the midst of persecution and brought Christians in that country through deep, deep waters. My first visit convinced me that persecution actually brings a depth of commitment that I almost envy. I'm not asking for persecution; I thank God for the freedom we have. But the Christians of Communist Romania knew what it meant to stand firm in faith no matter what enemies came against them.

That week in December 1989, Eugen and many other believers who had been praying for God's intervention saw the Lord answer their cries for help. God exists! And He was with His oppressed people in Romania.

– 9 –

RETURN TO ROMANIA

In the United States, we watched coverage of the Romanian revolution on television, although there was no way we could know everything that was happening in that country. I expected this stunning overthrow of the government would bring changes to the country, but I would not let it derail my plans to return to Romania—if we could get in. We were scheduled to leave in a few days, and we did not know exactly who was now in charge, if there would be travel restrictions, or if we might even be turned away. A friend called and advised that I should certainly go if I could. He counseled that the church would need me since many believers had been killed, the country was still in turmoil, and the future uncertain.

Another friend had made it possible for my son, David, to go with me. David was nine at the time, and we were both looking forward to this trip together. We were proceeding with our plans and both of us were packing to leave a few days after Christmas.

The night before our flight to Europe, the telephone rang. My friend Bill Overstreet, who had gone to Romania with me the year before, called to tell me he was praying for me, for a safe trip, and for God to use me in a mighty way.

Then he said, "Hey, Steve, you're not taking David, are you?"

"Oh, yeah. I'm planning to take him. We've haven't changed our plans."

"Steve, I don't think you should."

I said, "Thanks, Bill, but his way's been paid and we're looking forward to it."

He pressed, "I don't think you should take him."

"Well, thanks, but we are planning to go. Pray for us."

Two minutes after I hung up, the phone rang again. This time it was my friend from Pennsylvania, Ike Stoltzfus, who had also gone with me the year before. He told me he was praying for me and he too asked, "And you're not taking David, are you?"

"Well, yeah. I am."

"Steve, I don't think you should."

I had just finished the same conversation with Bill.

I asked Ike, "Have you been talking to Bill Overstreet?"

"No. Why?"

"Well, Bill just called and told me the same thing."

"I felt like the Lord told me to call you and say David shouldn't go," Ike explained.

How do you tell a nine-year-old boy who has his bags packed that he now must stay home? And how do you tell his dad that wise counsel from godly friends should be heeded? I wanted my son to go with me, but now I no longer had peace about taking him. And so Barb, Michelle, David, and I had a family conference.

"I really feel that the Lord's telling us something; and David, I just don't think you should go," I said. I was crying. David was crying. We were all crying.

Although our family all agreed on the final decision for David to stay home, I'll be very honest with you and tell you that I was angry for the first week of my trip. I was seeing the mighty hand of God doing unbelievable things, but I could not share that experience with my son.

In the days to come, I would be grateful that David was safe at home in Virginia, but God had to teach me first to accept that disappointment.

Four friends traveled with me this time. We flew into Vienna, still not certain we would be allowed to enter Romania. Feeling as though we needed a ticket to get us into the country, we found a fruit wholesaler and packed two Volkswagen vans with bananas and oranges.

As before, we drove first to Budapest, Hungary, where we spent the night. The next day we drove on to the Romanian border. The same guard that had stopped us the year before walked up to my window as I stopped the car.

"Do you have any arms or ammunition?"

"No."

"Do you have drugs?"

"No."

"Pornography?"

"No."

"Welcome to free Romania," he said, smiling.

"I've got a Bible, though. Do you want one?" I asked. He took the Bible and kissed the cover. I gave him an orange and he accepted it as though it were a treasure. We handed out oranges to all the guards. It was a precious, precious moment.

At the same hotel we'd stayed in the year before, we walked in and heard the "Hallelujah Chorus" coming from the television set. I lost it, right then and there, and stood in the lobby with tears running down my face.

"Sir, are you OK?" asked the lady at the desk.

"He just loves Romania," one of my friends said.

I gave the lady an orange, and I will cherish the memory of that moment as long as I live. I'm sure she had never seen an orange before. She held it in her hands as though it were a piece of gold. She put it to her nose and took a deep breath. "I see pictures," she said, "and always wonder what one smells like."

I took it from her and began to peel it.

"No! No!" she cried. "I want to show my family!"

"I'll give you another one for your family." I finished peeling it and gave it back to her. She sat there and wept. I guessed her to be forty-five years old, and she had never seen an orange!

I remembered buying coffee during my previous trip to Timişoara. First Baptist Church was building a new church. When I spoke there, they were still in the old building but had somehow obtained permission from the government to build a new meeting place. The people of First Baptist were doing most of the work themselves, coming after their usual workday was finished and spending many more hours laboring on their new church. I promised to buy coffee for those who worked, but coffee could only be purchased at the "dollar stores." As an American, I could shop in these stores selling "luxuries" like coffee. Romanians could not buy there; only those with American dollars or German marks and a valid passport were allowed entrance. The luxuries on the shelves were not for Romanians. That's a small example of the repression the Romanian people lived under for decades.

So I had made a trip to the dollar store. Coffee was packaged by the pound, wrapped in yellow plastic, and sold in cartons of twenty-four packs. The packs looked like bars of gold and were probably just as precious to those who could not buy coffee. I bought six of those cartons of gold and was carrying them out of the store when a lady said to me, "Sir, I fear for your life."

God was doing amazing things all across Romania. We went first to Oradea, then to Cluj, and arrived in Timişoara on January 11. Turmoil and fear still churned through the city. Bursts of gunfire sometimes came from rooftops, and no one seemed to know who was shooting. Rumors raised the alarm that the Securitate had simply gone underground but now was going to take back control. No one felt safe or certain of the future.

I spoke at First Baptist on Sunday morning and again in the evening. After the evening service, I went to the home of one of the pastors to have dinner and throughout our meal we heard gunshots and army vehicles moving about. What was happening out there in Timişoara's streets? Was the war breaking out again? My friend Ed Scearce had spoken at another church that night; where was he now? Was he safe?

I felt an urgency to return to the hotel, but was it safe for me to travel in the city? My hosts were reluctant to go out. "I've gotta get back," I insisted. They finally agreed and we ventured through the streets, not knowing what we might drive into.

We reached the hotel and found it surrounded by army vehicles. I was stopped, but when I showed my hotel key, I was allowed to go in. Ed was already there.

We debated. We had no idea why these armed men were outside; we weren't even sure who they were. Might we be caught in an attack? Timişoara is not too far from the Hungarian border. Should we make a run for it? How could we do that? Did we have a chance of getting through the lines of army tanks? Should we try to find a way out of the city? Should we stay? Gunshots punched through our conversation and the rumbling of tanks and trucks rolled around the building as we talked and prayed.

God invaded the room with His presence. We knew God wanted us here. He had brought us here and we would stay. We had no idea what the night would bring, but God gave us peace.

I turned over and went to sleep.

The banging on the door jolted fear through my heart and body. I sat up in bed and saw it was three o'clock in the morning.

"Meester Weengfield, Meester Weengfield!" someone was calling through my door.

"Yes?" I answered.

"Your friend, Ken Weaver, Ken Weaver from Harrisonburg, Virginia."

A voice with a heavy accent and broken English was talking to me about Harrisonburg, Virginia? Was I dreaming this conversation? Was I in some sort of trance?

"What?"

"Meester Weengfield. Ken Weaver. Men-no-nite Media."

I had not talked with anyone at home for almost a week. At that time in Romania, we could only contact the States by first calling the operator, making a reservation for a call to be made, and then waiting until they made the call for us. And by "waiting" I mean waiting for days. It might be as long as two days before a call would come back from the operator saying that my call was now going through. As a result, we had very little communication with the States while we were in Romania.

But Ken Weaver, who was then head of Mennonite Media, had called my wife, Barb, to find out where I was. He had contacted a Hungarian television crew making a documentary in Romania for British Broadcasting and asked them to find me and interview me. They wanted my perspective on what was happening in the country and what I was seeing. So at three in the morning, I opened the door and taped the interview.

By four I was back in bed; but at five, someone was banging on my door again. This time, the representative of the governor of Timişoara stood in the hallway. A special service would be held that day to remember those who had been killed in the revolution. Would I speak as a representative of America?

The service was held at the city center where the revolution had begun. Peter Dugalescu went with me. The city bore the scars of battles, and as we walked down the steps of the Orthodox cathedral, I thought of the young people who had been massacred there. A group of young men had marched to the cathedral carrying a Romanian flag with a hole in the center and, in brave voices, sang a national song banned by the government. They had been cut down by gunfire, and many died.

All over the city, Romanian flags had a wide circle cut into the yellow panel. Under Ceauşescu's regime, a coat of arms had been added to the country's flag and the emblem had come to represent the Communist government. That insignia was cut out during the days of revolution, and the blue, yellow, and red flags now unfurled in the wind with the hole in the center announcing the nation's freedom from tyranny.

An estimated sixty-five thousand people had gathered in the city center, and the ceremony was being televised to the entire country. When it was my turn to speak, I called everyone's attention to the flags flying from tanks and army vehicles, from cars and buses and buildings—all of the flags had that hole at the center.

"What will now fill that space in your country and your lives?" I challenged them. "Communism has been cut out of Romania, but what will take its place? If the void is filled with materialism and greed, you'll be just as empty as you were under Communism." I preached the gospel, Peter translated for me, and the ears of the entire country heard the message: "Romania's only hope is to fill the void with Jesus Christ."

The Orthodox choir sang a song that to my ears sounded very much like a funeral dirge. As they finished, a burst of gunfire crackled through the air, echoing off the walls of the centuries-old buildings.

My first thought was a prayer for help. *Oh, Lord! We've been attacked! Help us!*

Our minds work in crazy ways sometimes. My second reaction was gratitude that I was in the middle of the crowd, but my third thought was less comforting: I would probably be trampled to death in the panic.

A general standing next to me must have seen the fear in my face. "No problem," he reassured me. "Salute to the dead. Salute to the dead." Our military salutes in the United States are measured and synchronized. The gun salute that day in Romania was haphazard and disorganized.

Only seconds went by between the first sound of gunfire and the general's assurance that all was well; but those seconds, when I was sure we were under attack, were probably the most frightening moments of my life. I will never forget the bolt of terror that burned through me.

In spite of those frightening seconds, that day was a marvelous day, one of the most cherished memories of my life. God used my participation in that ceremony to introduce me to the entire country, opening the door for my ministry that continued for twenty-five years. God was doing amazing things in Romania, and it was such a joy to be a little part of the mending and healing of the hole in the blue, yellow, and red flag.

– 10 –

MIRACLES FOR
LONG BEACH .

$\sim\!\!\sim$

L et's adopt a city."
Luke Weaver was standing at my office door. He had just said to me, "We should do *something*."

I don't think he expected a suggestion that the *something* would be adopting a city.

It was August 26, 2005. The day before, Hurricane Katrina had hit southeast Florida and was now moving west into the Gulf of Mexico and gaining even more intensity. At the office, we had set up a TV in the conference room and were watching reports that were coming in from the Gulf Coast. I was back in my office when Luke came and stood at the door and said, "We should do something."

I felt the Lord spoke to me then, and the words came out: *Adopt a city*.

Most of the attention at that point was on New Orleans, but all along the coast, towns were being hit hard by Katrina. "Let's find a place that's been overlooked by everybody else, and let's go there and make a difference," I explained to Luke.

Where do you start when faced with such a huge need? I began to make calls to Rotary presidents in Mississippi, and one of the first I reached was the Rotary president in Hattiesburg. She owned a jewelry store, and her family was living in the store because of the damage to their home, but she pointed me to nearby towns where she said there had been real devastation—Long Beach, Gulfport, and one other town. She gave me the names of the Rotary presidents in each town; the first one I contacted was Bob Krantz in Long Beach.

Long Beach had been the epicenter of the storm, and they desperately needed help. Bob Krantz put me in touch with the mayor, and when I told him we felt that we should adopt his city, his response was, "We sure do need somebody to adopt us."

I was soon on the phone, making calls to church leaders, civic leaders, and government officials. That was Friday. We set up a breakfast meeting for Monday at Spotswood Country Club in Harrisonburg. Over a hundred people showed up. I cast the vision, and we divided into groups of about six to discuss what we could do. Karl Stoltzfus of Dynamic Aviation and Curt Hartman each volunteered to fly a delegation down to Long Beach on Wednesday of that week. Two planes flew us down, and we met with the mayor. We wanted to see the devastation firsthand so that we could come up with an effective plan to help.

As we flew into Gulfport, we could see rooftops covered with tarps, but the damage didn't seem too severe. We landed and drove over to the next town, Long Beach. When we crossed the railroad tracks that run through the town about half a mile from the waterfront, the scene looked like a tsunami or atomic bomb had hit. Everything from the railroad tracks to the beach was gone. It was absolute devastation.

After we returned to Virginia, I began calling the Long Beach mayor every day. Not many days had passed before he reported that they were in desperate need of food. Other relief drives had sent clothes and water, but people were standing in lines to get food—and there was very little to be had.

Albert, a friend in Bristol, Tennessee, runs a food bank. I called and asked for him and was told he was gone for a week.

"Where is he?" I asked, determined to talk with him even if he was on vacation.

"He's taken two tractor-trailer loads of food to the Gulf Coast."

God was days ahead of me!

I asked for Albert's cell number and called him. He had just pulled into Gulfport.

"Are those trucks committed?" I asked.

"No," he said. "We're looking for a distribution center."

"I've got one!"

He was just entering Gulfport on US-49. I knew where he was and was able to give him directions.

"Go until you see a Kangaroo station."

"I see it," he said.

"Take a right at the next intersection, go about two miles, and at the blinking light take a left. That's Klondyke Road. There's a fire station on the right. It's a distribution center, and they'll be waiting for you."

"I'll be there in a few minutes."

I hung up the phone and called the mayor.

"Billy, I've got two tractor trailers filled with food. They'll be there in about five minutes."

"Steve, this isn't a thing to kid about."

"I'm not kidding. It's a miracle, Billy. Get ready to unload the trucks!"

About three hours later, Billy called. I could tell he was crying. "Steve, I can't believe this!"

That was just the beginning of miracle after miracle that took place.

The owner of a company that makes sausage donated twelve thousand pounds and offered to take it down himself. We wanted to fill the truck, so Purdue added twelve thousand pounds of chicken breasts and Virginia Poultry Growers gave twelve thousand pounds of turkey. As the truck rolled into the Long Beach area, I called my friend who was driving the truck. He picked up, but for a moment he couldn't talk. When he could, he choked out, "Thank you for giving me the privilege of bringing this down here."

Over the next several months, we took at least two more tractor-trailer loads of food. A company in Michigan heard what we were doing and gave us two loads of furniture that went to firemen, police officers, and teachers who had lost everything in the storm. The school in Long Beach had lost its gymnasium so we took our tent down and set it up. It's the size of a football field, and for one year, the school used it as their activity center. For over two years, we sent teams down every two weeks. We rebuilt homes. We raised over two million dollars for the city.

God was showing up in everything. It was all His doing—like the new day care center for the city. They needed a new facility for day care so that people could go back to work. One day, I was over in Greenwood, Delaware, and as I was driving down the road, I saw a sign for Beracah Homes. I stopped, went into their reception area, and asked for the owner.

He happened to be standing close by and said, "I'm the owner."

I introduced myself and told him about our relief effort in Long Beach, Mississippi, and their need for a day care center. "And I was wondering if you could give us one."

His answer to that bold request?

"I've been praying about what I could do. I'll do it. I'll give you one." The building was worth almost $200,000, and Beracah Homes took it down to Long Beach and set it up for the city.

I thank God for all those miracles that took place.

As time went on, I really felt the Lord call me to give them a festival, a gift to the community. We set up our tent and did a festival crusade in Long Beach. Randy Travis, Ricky Skaggs, Nicole C. Mullen, and my good friend John Schmid were special guests. It was a great week, and many people came to Christ or recommitted their lives. The crusade cost the ministry about $200,000, but friends made it possible, and it gave the Long Beach community hope.

In the three years of our "adoption," miracle after miracle took place. We made friends and we made a difference. I'm thankful to God for all that took place, and I'm thankful for the difference that Christ's church made in Long Beach, Mississippi.

VICTORY WEEKEND

In the early 2000s, we held a festival in Bristol, Tennessee. We were at Viking Hall Civic Center for eight nights; it was a wonderful week, and God showed up in a major way. The city's downtown has a unique main street—half of it is in Tennessee, and the other half is in Virginia. As you walk down State Street, the center line on the pavement is the state line. Bristol, Tennessee, is on the south side of the street; Bristol, Virginia, is on the north.

Bristol, of course, is also the home of Bristol Motor Speedway. Although I had never been to a NASCAR race, I had followed auto racing and knew what was going on. This was done more as a witnessing opportunity than anything else; if somebody wanted to talk about racing, I wanted to be able to discuss it with some degree of knowledge and intelligence. I'd also met two of the Wood brothers of the Wood Brothers Racing team. We'd done a crusade in Stuart, Virginia, the home of the Wood brothers. One night during the crusade, Delano Wood, one of the founding brothers, responded to the invitation and gave his life to Christ. That experience was even more wonderful because that night Delano was led to Christ by his brother Ray Lee, who was a Christian and trained to share his faith as a counselor in our crusade.

So I've known about NASCAR, followed it, and enjoyed it, but had never been to a race. During the week of our festival in Bristol, the general manager of the speedway, Jeff Byrd, was on our crusade committee, and he invited me to come out and see the Speedway. I even got to drive on the track.

As a result of that, I was invited to do a chapel service on a Sunday morning at the racetrack. I came out of the chapel that day and looked at one hundred sixty thousand fans sitting around a half-mile track, and as an evangelist, I began to froth at the mouth. *There's gotta be a way to do something here*, I thought. I started praying about possibilities at Bristol, but I would pray for years before anything happened.

After praying about it for so long, one day I just picked up the phone, called the racetrack, and asked to speak to the general manager. Jeff Byrd had died of pancreatic cancer in 2010, and I was transferred to Jerry Caldwell, the new general manager. I introduced myself, told him I was an evangelist, and explained that I'd like to talk with him about doing "something" during race week. We set an appointment, and I drove down to Bristol to meet him.

"We've met before," Jerry said soon after I'd entered his office and greeted him.

"We have?" I didn't know where or when. I didn't remember him.

"Yeah, at the golf shop in Pinehurst."

Then I did remember him. I had been speaking at a men's event and golf outing at Pinehurst in North Carolina. Waiting for my tee time, I was talking to someone in the golf shop and sharing my faith. As we finished our conversation, another gentleman came over and asked if I was from Southwest Virginia. He'd noticed my golf shirt, from a very nice course in Southwest Virginia. I told him no, I'd been a guest at that Virginia club with a friend of mine. Our conversation went no further; my tee time was called and I had to leave. I had never talked with the man (Jerry, it turned out) again, but in the providence of God, we had met that day, and God had lined things up for our meeting now in Bristol.

When Jerry heard what I wanted to do, he was immediately on board. "Let's do it."

It was late spring, and I had been thinking about doing a festival in the spring of the next year, a year away. Jerry, though, said, "No, let's do it in August."

"Well, OK!" I agreed. But that gave us only three months to pull off a full-fledged festival.

A person heard about what we were doing and wanted to partner with us. He said it could be a money-making event, and we could get sponsorship to pay for everything. Well, we'd never done that before, but it sounded intriguing. If I can preach the gospel and we can make money, I guess it would be OK. I said yes to his offer.

Our new partner recommended a person who would raise the sponsorship, so I hired him and agreed to pay him per diem. For almost three months, we were busy planning, and I didn't pay too much attention to what we were getting in sponsorship, but our fundraiser said things were going well.

Then we were within a week of the beginning of the event. We'd planned a full-fledged festival. The stage was set up at the dragstrip, and it was going to be a major event. We were going to be streaming live on Facebook. Our first event would be on Wednesday night.

The Friday before the start of the festival, I talked with the person raising our money. He said we had a major sponsor contributing $50,000, and he would have to go up to Connecticut to pick up the check. He was first going to Nashville, where he'd get another $25,000 from each of four record labels, and we had $10,000 from a marina down in Johnson City, Tennessee. I was doing the math, and I thought, *$160,000. We're done. It's all being paid!* Even better, he thought if he stayed in Nashville through Monday, he could pick up another $50,000.

We're fifty thousand to the good! OK!

But I needed money immediately to pay the bills, and I asked him to FedEx what he already had.

The weekend went by. Monday came, and there was nothing from FedEx. I called him, and he explained he had just got tied up and didn't get the money sent.

I needed that money. When I left home, my dad said, "Son, I gave you a good name. You take care of it." I've done my best to live up to that, and I've made it a point to never leave town after a crusade owing anybody anything.

I was firm. "Get the money to us! We need it now!"

"OK," he said. "I'll do it right now."

Tuesday came. We received nothing. And there was no word from our fundraiser.

He had said he'd be on his way to Bristol by Wednesday morning. He never showed up.

Opening night for the festival was Wednesday evening. Fifteen minutes before I was to walk on stage to speak to about seven hundred youth, I got a phone call and the man admitted to me, "I don't have anything."

"What do you mean you don't have anything?"

"I was speaking in faith," he said.

"No, you were lying!"

I walked over to where Facebook was set up in an air-conditioned area. The August day was hot and I was sweaty and worn out. I called the person who had wanted to partner with us and had agreed to pay half of the expenses. I gave him the news: We didn't have one sponsor.

"What do you mean?"

"He's raised nothing. We have nothing. We're $160,000 in the hole."

That was his cue to exit the partnership too.

I would have to take out an equity line on our home and pay the bills because I wasn't going to leave town until people were paid. Was

I discouraged? Yes, without question. But I still had hope because I put my faith and trust in Jesus that we'd be able to pay this off.

What happened was wrong. The people who were involved are going to have to stand before God one day and give an account. I've forgiven them, and I pray for them. And life has gone on.

I went on stage that night and shared the gospel with seven hundred young people. We had a great night, and many responded to the gospel. It was a successful youth night. But on Saturday and Sunday, there was almost no one in the stands. The crowd was sparse, only one hundred people at the most.

This first event at Bristol was when we learned how not to do it. For one thing, we were at the dragstrip. The sparse crowds told me that the fans were not going to come to the dragstrip, they were over at the track, so we needed to go there. The youth night was successful, and I'm thankful for all the young people who got saved on Wednesday night. The Facebook live stream reached people who will never be at Bristol—we heard from Romania, Russia, Africa, Europe, and all over the United States—but the stands at the dragstrip were basically empty. Saturday and Sunday were a bust if you looked at the numbers.

The word for all of us is, "And let us not be weary in well doing: for in due season we shall reap, if we faint not" (Galatians 6:9 KJV). I could have thrown in the towel and said, "Man, this was a crazy thing to do, this NASCAR thing. What a dumb idea." I could have been defeated by the disappointing numbers and the failure of the sponsorship plan. But God opened my eyes to see what might be. This first NASCAR outreach did not work, but I knew it *could* work. God had birthed a vision in me.

In the last ten years, what God has done through our Victory Weekends at Bristol Motor Speedway has been phenomenal. We moved from Bristol to Darlington, South Carolina; Dover, Delaware;

Daytona, Florida; Michigan; and other places. We have seen thousands of people come to faith in Christ, and we've honored veterans and active-duty military. I could tell you story after story after story of people who have responded to our services and touched my heart.

Here are three of those stories. I share them because they happened three weekends in a row and powerfully impacted my life.

I'm also sharing them to raise awareness of the suicide issue among veterans and active-duty military. We need to pray for them, regardless of what our position is on military service. Our country has multiple generations of people who have been damaged by war, and if the church can't speak into their lives, something is wrong with the church. Over these last years, our ministry has worked at reaching them to offer healing and hope in Jesus's name.

At one event, we had about one hundred eighty veterans who came forward at my invitation. We honored them, and many, many people prayed to receive Christ. When I came off the platform, there was a gentleman my age who literally fell into my arms; if I had not hugged him and held him up, he would have fallen to the ground. He was weeping uncontrollably, but when he finally got control of himself, he said, "Thank you, sir. Thank you."

"Sir, thank *you*," I replied.

He shared this with me: "When I came back from Vietnam, people yelled at me, they cursed me, they spit on me. This is the first time in forty years that I've felt honored."

I prayed with him.

When our conversation was finished and I turned, I saw a young man of about nineteen standing there. Tears ran down his face.

"What's wrong, son?" I asked.

"You nailed me to the wall, preacher."

"What do you mean?"

He explained. "I got back from Afghanistan three weeks ago, and I've thought of nothing but suicide every day. I was going to come to the race this weekend and pull the trigger on Monday, but Jesus rescued me tonight."

I prayed with him too.

The next weekend, I was preaching at the one hundredth anniversary of a Methodist church not far from where I live. They held the event in a rented community center because they expected a large crowd. During the service, I did what I usually do—I asked, "Do we have any veterans here?" Wherever I see the first hand go up, I ask that person to come forward and I put a medal around their neck and explain that this is what we do at the racetrack in honor of our veterans. At this service, I called up a veteran who raised his hand, and I medaled him. And the service went on.

After the service, the guest praise band was packing up, and the drummer, a young man, approached me.

"Hey, you keep doing what you're doing, man," he said.

"I plan to."

Then he said, "I should be a statistic."

I asked him to tell me his story.

He was also a veteran. Several years before, he had taken a 9-mm handgun and shot himself in the head, but he survived. Through that experience, he came to faith in Christ. I've shared his story ever since because it so impacted my life.

The third weekend, I was preaching at a large church in Lynchburg and again asked how many veterans were in the audience. A hand went up, I had the man come forward, and I medaled him. He was a Vietnam veteran. He went back to his seat, but I noticed that all during the service, he was weeping. After the service ended, he came back up to me and said, "I guess you're wondering what's going on."

"Yes, I am," I said.

He explained his tears: his son had served in Iraq, returned home, and then killed himself.

Three weekends in a row! The baggage of these wars that we've been involved in is unconscionable. Our service men and women have been exposed to things that no human being should ever have to go through. Some have been deployed multiple times, over and over again. The son of a good friend was deployed for the twelfth or thirteenth time. Just before he boarded the plane the last time, he told his dad, "I know if I keep going over there, Dad, I'm gonna get it." He was killed by a sniper.

That's what's going on in our world, and we can't ignore it. We need to help these individuals who have been so wounded and damaged by war, and our ministry is doing whatever we can to strengthen and encourage them.

I thank God for what He's doing through Victory Weekends, and we will not stop or be defeated by discouragement.

– 12 –

WHEN BEARS ATTACK

David Wingfield

I was delighted when my dad asked me to write a chapter for his book on faith. I knew immediately that I would tell the following story. It's a bit different than the other stories you've read so far, but it definitely belongs in this book. The bottom line is it takes faith to go on a hike with Steve Wingfield.

❖

2:05 a.m.	An Appalachian black bear attacks my father.
2:06 a.m.	I undergo the most horrific experience of my thirty-four years of existence.
2:08 a.m.	My coworker loses control of his bowels.
2:20 a.m.	Deaf Bob presumed dead—the Appalachian Trail killer is on the loose!

It was summer and my dad and I were on our yearly section hike of the Appalachian Trail. A coworker (we'll call him "Kyle" for the sake of anonymity) joined us to make it three. On the trail we connected with another section hiker named Bob. I met Bob on the trail and said, "Hello." He kept hiking. There was the off chance he hadn't heard me, so I shouted "HELLO!" in my loud-yet-still-friendly hiker voice. No pause, no change of pace. After a few eerie moments of hiking alone in the woods with someone who would not acknowledge my existence, he saw me. He stopped. I stopped. "HI," he said, "MY NAME IS BOB. I'M VERY DEAF." Everything Bob said was very loud. Bob fished around in his shirt pocket for some hearing aids. "I CAN HEAR YOU IF I PUT IN THESE SPECIALIZED HEARING AIDS, BUT I DON'T LIKE TO WEAR THEM WHEN I'M SLEEPING, HIKING, OR IN THE WOODS." We said a few words and then Bob stuffed them back into his pocket. I gave the thumbs-up sign and smiled. We were hiking in the woods, so that was that.

The plan was to set camp at the Dismal Falls campground where some Crazy shot two hikers a few years back. The hikers later said he was acting funny. (Hikers have a morbid sense of humor.) The hikers were wounded but escaped alive. The Crazy went to jail.

When you're hiking in the woods, you try not to think about the whole crazy-person-who-tries-to-kill-you-in-the-woods scenario. The problem is that your brain keeps circling back to the thing you're working hard at not thinking about. It isn't good to hike alone with your fears; fear is better shared:

Me:	"Remember that guy who shot those hikers at Dismal?"
Kyle:	"The Dismal Falls we're hiking to?"
Pops:	"They were just wounded."
Kyle:	"Is there more than one Dismal Falls?"
Me:	"There's only one Dismal."

We hiked to Dismal in silence. Of course, Deaf Bob always hikes in silence.

A knee-deep stream cuts through Dismal Campground, leading to the namesake falls, a noisy eight-footer. After supper, Deaf Bob put in his ears to say he would "SET UP ON THE FAR SIDE OF

THIS CREEK" and "SEE YOU GUYS IN THE MORNING." Kyle pitched his one-man on the near side of the creek and Dad and I put our two-man twenty yards further down.

2:05 a.m. Dismal Falls, Virginia

My dad wakes. A bear rustles against the tent. A black bear could rip through a tent like a bear opening a can of sardines. OK—bad analogy. Time slows. My dad thinks about life, the universe, his wife, his son asleep beside him and who may die with him on this lonesome night at Dismal Falls. My dad is a man of action. He attacks the bear.

"HEY!" he screams. "GET OUT!" He rolls on his side and starts punching the bear though the wall of the tent. His fists slam into the thick animal, but the bear won't leave—it starts fighting back. He hears me yell, "Dad!" His son's voice gives him a surge of paternal energy. He gives the bear everything he has. "GIT!"

I slept through my dad's first shout of "HEY!" The sleeping stopped when he screamed "GET OUT!" and started hitting me. "Dad!" I yelled. My dad used to be a cop and even in his sixties he's no softy. "GIT!" I struggled to free myself from my mummy bag. "Dad," I pleaded, "stop!"

"GET! OUT! OF! HERE!" my dad yelled, punctuating each word with a fist. "THERE'S A BEAR!" My dad must be dreaming. "Wake up!" I freed my hands and tried to block the punches, my eyes adjusting to the moonlight. My father screamed, "I AM AWAKE!"

I saw the wild whites of his eyes. He wasn't dreaming. Fear, pain, and animal self-preservation exploded from the base of my brain. As Isaac looked into the eyes of Father Abraham, sacrificial knife held high, so I looked into the eyes of my father and felt my universe spin into implosion—my father was insane. After a lifetime of love and laughter it came down to this one night in a two-man tent. One of us would get out alive. The door was on his side. My dad is thirty-three years my senior and he's had a good life, so in the strictly utilitarian sense of equality . . . he had to die. It isn't easy to get to the mental place of being morally OK with beating your father to death, or at least senseless enough so you can crawl over him and unzip the tent door, but him going insane and trying to kill you is a good place to start.

I rolled into him with my body to shorten his punches and tried to reason with whatever kernel of sanity remained. "There. Is. No. Bear." I grabbed his up-side wrist and pinned it to his body.

"Then what has my arm?"

"I do!" I assured him. His body loosened.

"There's no bear. It's just me."

"I guess . . . I thought you were a bear."

My dad started to chuckle. It was infectious. There's a lot to laugh about when your dad stops trying to kill you.

"You can really hit," I said.

"Sorry. I thought the door was on my left side."

"I turned the bags around when you did your last pee."

"Oh."

"I'm glad you didn't get up in the middle of the night to pee out the door."

"You're lucky I was just trying to kill you."

"Do you think Kyle heard us yelling?"

"If he's worried he'll come check on us."

2:08 a.m. Kyle hears the yelling in the dark of night and loses control of an essential bodily function.

Kyle woke to hear only four shouts in the Dismal darkness: "HEY!" . . . "GET OUT!" . . . "GIT!" . . . "GET OUT OF HERE!" Then silence—silence, the eternal rushing of water, and the roar of his own heart. The Killer was back. Instinctively, Kyle's body loosened what could be loosened in preparation for fight or flight. In common hiking parlance this is referred to as "dropping weight." Kyle scrambled out of his tent and yanked down his white spandex thermals. He perched there, birdlike and shivering, for fifteen minutes. The killer was looking for him. Reason says: "If you don't want a psycho killer to find you in the woods, don't crouch in front of your tent over a mound of fresh poo while wearing full-body semi-reflective white spandex." Reason is not terror's first advisor and Kyle was terrified. But he didn't want to die here, not like this. He stood, pulled up his spandex, switched on his headlamp and waded barefoot across the creek. Deaf Bob was probably dead. He swept his light across Bob's tent, expecting slash marks and blood. Nothing. Maybe Bob was OK. "Bob!?" No response. Bob was dead. Kyle crept around the tent, inspecting each side with his light. The tent was fine . . . then it moved. Kyle froze. Once again terror flushed through his body but this time there was nothing left to flush. Bob stuck his head into the light.

"WHAT THE HECK!?"

"Are you OK?" No reply.

"HANG ON . . . LET ME PUT MY EARS IN."

Kyle waited.

"WHAT'S GOING ON?"

"It's me, Kyle."

"OK."

"Did you hear something in the night?"

"I'M DEAF."

"I heard some yelling."

" . . . "

"So you're OK?"

"YEP."

"What was it?"

"I DON'T KNOW. I'M DEAF. GO TO SLEEP."

Kyle waded back across the creek and crawled into his sleeping bag. He couldn't sleep. The morning brought relief but he had to watch his step while packing up. We never got Deaf Bob's take on Midnight Kyle. He left in the morning at the first road we crossed.

"I'M HEADING IN."

"I thought you were out for the weekend?"

"NOT ANYMORE."

"Where does that road go?"

"I'LL FIND OUT." Bob removed his ears and walked on.

After Bob left, Kyle got sort of quiet. "How did you all sleep last night?"

"It was Dismal."

– 13 –

MIRACLE ON · THE MOUNTAIN

~

In August of 2015, my good friend Jeff Bowers called me and said, "I have a piece of property I want you to look at."

"Jeff, I don't have money to buy a property. I'm a preacher."

"I feel like the Lord wants you to see this," he replied.

How could I argue with that? Besides, I knew I'd enjoy spending time with Jeff and being outdoors.

I met my friend at his office in Franklin, West Virginia, and he had an ATV on the back of his truck. We climbed in, and he drove out to the property in the mountains. The lane went up a pretty steep incline and twisted through several switchbacks. We offloaded the ATV and drove it up to the rim of what looks like a big bowl. Held in the shelter of this bowl was an old farmhouse, a stand-alone garage, a storage building, and three ponds that are spring fed. The 524 acres had once been a farm, nestled in the mountains of Pendleton County, West Virginia.

As I got my first view from the ridge looking down into the bowl, it was almost as though I heard the Lord speaking in an audible voice, saying, "This property belongs to Paul Weaver." Paul and his wife, Gladys, have been friends of mine for well over thirty years and supporters of the ministry.

I didn't tell Jeff what I was sure I'd heard. But I did say, "I think I might know who will want this property."

We spent the morning exploring the property, the fields and forest on the mountainside behind the farm. We saw deer and turkey and signs of bear, and I enjoyed our time together.

The next day, I called Paul and said, "Paul I don't know what this is about, but a friend of mine wanted me to look at some property. I went out and looked at it and felt like the Lord said it belongs to you."

He interrupted me.

"Wingfield! I got cold chills when you said that. Gladys and I are looking for property. We're leaving Thursday to go to Canada. She didn't want to go; it's too far away. I'm going to cancel Canada and I'll come down on Monday."

We met at Jeff's office in Franklin and drove out to the property. Jeff had already taken two ATVs out. Paul and Gladys got on one ATV, and Jeff and I were on the other.

Paul was seeing the vision even before we had explored the entire property. "This is unbelievable!" he said. "It's everything I've dreamed of."

Gladys said, "I'm not easily impressed, but I'm impressed."

We spent the morning checking out the property. Jeff's wife had packed us a picnic lunch, and while we were eating, Paul pointed up toward the rim of the bowl and said, "That's where I'm going to put the first house."

"We need to commit that to the Lord," I said, so we drove up to the spot he'd pointed out, got off the ATVs, and knelt down right there. I prayed a prayer of commitment.

Then Paul stood up and took out a snake pistol he was carrying; he pointed it in the direction of the mountain and emptied it. Then he turned to me and said, "Steve, I don't want this property. I just want to have access to it. Why don't I write a check to the ministry, and you buy this land. We'll build a retreat here for the pastors and veterans you're trying to help."

That's where it all started.

The lady who was selling it heard that we wanted to build a retreat on the property; her husband, who was deceased, had been a veteran. She reduced her asking price, and Jeff gave up his commission. My friends Paul and Gladys wrote us a check, and we paid cash for the property.

The first house was built on the spot where we had prayed a prayer of commitment to the Lord. The material—the stone, windows, siding, doors, roof, lumber, excavation, everything—was donated.

That fall, I was on my way to preach at our Victory Weekend event at Bristol Motor Speedway. En route I saw a stack of logs at an exit off I-81. They were for sale with a telephone number, and I said to myself, "Those would make a nice chapel for the retreat center." I didn't have time to stop, and after the race I was going somewhere else to preach, so I went home a different way. For the next year, I looked for that stack of logs but never found them. I thought I'd seen them somewhere in Southwest Virginia, so it appeared that they were gone. *Someone has probably bought them*, I told myself.

In July of 2017, I saw the logs again! They were stacked up on the side of the road about twenty-five miles south of our home. This time, I pulled in, got the number, and called the seller, Brandon Traylor.

"I've been trying to sell those logs for a year," Brandon told me.

I said, "Well, I believe the Lord saved them for me."

"I could have sold them before," said Brandon, "but people just want to make flooring out of them. I want them to find a home."

"I've got a home for them. I want them to be a chapel."

That sparked his interest. I invited him to come over to the property and take a look at the spot where I wanted to build the chapel. And then we'd talk about buying the logs. I gave him directions.

The next Monday, I was sitting on the patio of the first house we had built, having a cup of coffee when Brandon and his partner, Jason, drove up. The first thing Brandon said to me when he got out of his truck was, "My wife said, 'God brought you into my life for such a time as this.'"

"I need to meet her. I like the way she thinks."

"She also told me not to rip you off."

"Brandon, you wouldn't be ripping me off, you'd be ripping God off—and you don't want to go there!"

We went down to the spot where I envisioned a chapel at the heart of the property, adjacent to an old cemetery.

"I'll tell you what, preacher," he said. "I paid $12,000 for those logs, and I'll sell 'em to you for $12,000. And I'll put up the chapel for you."

I stuck out my hand. "We got a deal."

Then I said, "Let's go down and look at the old farmhouse. Part of that building is also a log house, and I can see renovating and enlarging it but keeping its character. Do the chapel and maybe I will get you to do the farmhouse."

We went down to the farmhouse, and I explained what I wanted to do. Jason chimed in.

"I took a barn down a year ago, and I'll let you have that lumber to add on here and keep this history intact."

The two were busy measuring everything, and I went up to the house to make lunch for all of us. A little while later they came up.

"This has been an awesome day, guys," I said. "I've got my chapel, and you're going to give me material to add on to the farmhouse. I may as well tell you my other dream. I want to put a barn up here as an event center so we can have youth groups up here."

Jason spoke up. "A man in Pennsylvania had asked me to take down his barn, but he wanted quite a bit of money for it."

"Where is the barn?" I asked.

"Chambersburg."

"We did a crusade in Chambersburg. The guy might know me," I said.

Jason didn't think there was much chance of that, but he agreed to give the man a call.

The next day I was at the office when Jason called. I answered the phone, and he was crying.

"What's going on, man?" I asked him.

"I've never been a part of anything like this," he said.

He went on to tell me that he had called the man in Chambersburg, a Mr. Miller, and told him that he had found a place for his barn—and that he thought we might know each other. Mr. Miller asked, "What's his name?" Jason gave him my name.

The phone went silent. Then the man on the other end said, "I'm sitting here wearing a T-shirt that Steve Wingfield gave me twelve years ago. He was having a crusade here, and I helped put up the tent. You tell Steve he can have the barn."

When Jason finished with his story, I asked for Mr. Miller's phone number and called him immediately. Then I changed everything on my schedule for the rest of the day and drove to Chambersburg and took him and his wife out to lunch.

"Steve," he said during lunch, "it's the craziest thing. I had not worn that T-shirt since forever. The night before, I looked at it and thought, *Oh, I'll put this on and pray for Steve tonight.* And the next morning while I'm wearing it, I got this phone call about a barn you can use."

This is what has been happening over and over again at the Lodestar Mountain Inn. We've had ten tractor-trailer loads of material donated to us. Brandon and Jason took down the barn in Pennsylvania and brought it to the mountain. We had put in the foundation and the subfloor and were ready to get started on the barn.

It was the last day of hunting season, and Brandon was in Augusta County, Virginia, up in his tree stand. His phone rang, and someone said, "Somebody's taking down that house you're interested in."

Brandon had seen a log house that was abandoned. Several times he had tried calling the owner, but no one answered or returned his call. Now, the house was being taken down.

He grabbed all his hunting gear, crawled down out of his tree stand, and drove over to the house.

When Brandon drove up to the house he recognized the man. When Brandon walked into the house, they made eye contact and the man said, "I was going to call you first. I just wanted the money to take it down. If you want the logs you can have them."

Brandon said, "I think I have a home for them."

Brandon called me immediately. "You want it?"

"Yeah, let's get it!" I said.

The house was built in 1830 as a miller's house. With nine-foot ceilings on both the first and second floors, it was a very rare find. You just don't find any log cabins like that. It was moved to the Lodestar Mountain Inn and we started work on that building. It's now finished and furnished, has five bedrooms, and is absolutely gorgeous. It is a testimony to what we want to see happen to people who come to the Lodestar Mountain Inn. Just like the barn and the log house that were ready for the burn pile, they have been restored and that is what God wants to do to lives that have been shattered by the battles of life. God is now at work at the Lodestar Mountain Inn restoring lives.

Then we went back to work on the barn. A friend from Sarasota, Florida, Bob Detweiler, whom I had led to Christ a number of years ago, said he would pay someone to put the barn up for us. He had been raised Amish, and he found an Amish barn builder from Kidron, Ohio. The builder and his crew came down in the fall, and the frame of the barn was soon up and braced. The crew went home for Thanksgiving and were going to return the next week to finish up.

On the Monday morning after Thanksgiving, I got a phone call. A wind shear had come through over the weekend, and the barn was down. It was totally destroyed.

I called Abe, the Amish builder. He was devastated, as we all were. He came down the next week and cleaned up the site. "I'm going to find us another barn," he said.

Sure enough, he found a barn near Orville, Ohio. He and his crew took it down and brought it to the Lodestar Mountain Inn. "This barn's better," he joked, "because it came from Ohio." That barn is now up and ready for events. It also has five bedrooms in it. The log house, which we call the Evangel House, also has five bedrooms; the first house built has five bedrooms; and we have two cottages with two bedrooms in each. We're ready!

This is how it all started. God's been mighty good to us. It's been almost unbelievable, except that I believe it, because our God can do mighty things.

Why is this place called the Lodestar Mountain Inn?

A number of years ago, I was asked to be involved with Lodestar Guidance, a leadership development character-building program that originated under the leadership of Paul Weaver at his company, Weaver Leather. The *lodestar* is the guiding star that leads or guides, and this program presents guiding principles for character development and leadership. The North Star is also called the lodestar; the mountain behind us is North Mountain. The lodestar is the navigational star, and the Lodestar Mountain Inn is located in one of the darkest places on the east coast. People come from all over just to see the night sky.

In His providence, God has put all this together, and we are praying this place is going to be a place of healing and hope and restoration for pastors, veterans, and others who've been damaged by the struggles of life.

Without question, it's all been a miracle on the mountain.

This Book Is Dedicated to the Most Important People in My Life

I have a wonderful team, and there's no way that I could do what I do or have done without their support. A special thank-you goes to my executive assistant and partner in ministry who is an evangelist herself. I've been honored to work with Terry Wyant-Vargo for more than twenty years, and I thank God for her faithful service to Jesus! To her husband, Thomas, who thinks we're both crazy, and he is correct: we are crazy in love with Jesus. Our executive team is also made up of Luke Weaver, who serves as Director of Lodestar Guidance and Ministry Relations, Scott Wenger, Director of Lodestar Mountain Inn, and his wife, Associate Director Amy Wenger. Sara Ferrell, Delphos Howard, Nicole Wright, Jeff Wilhelm, Jessica Taylor, and Corey Friel make up the remainder of the team.

I also dedicate this work to my family. Barb, who has been my companion for almost forty-nine years, has put up with my dreams and my passion to use every available means to reach every available person. A crazy schedule and many nights spent alone while I was somewhere in the world preaching the gospel have not been easy, and I could not have experienced much of this without her prayers and support.

To my daughter, Michelle Wingfield Curlin, and her husband, Howard. They support me, they encourage me, and most importantly, they pray for me. They believe in my mission in life to proclaim Christ! They have blessed me with six wonderful grandchildren, Phin, Lars, Katie Anne, Field, Jude, and J. R.

To my son, David, and his wife, Havi. They support me, they encourage me, and most importantly, they pray for me. They believe in my mission in life to proclaim Christ. They have blessed me with two wonderful grandchildren, Selah and Jubal.

My mom and dad, Floyd and Annie Wingfield, have been with Jesus for many years. I thank God for the faithful example they modeled for me and all my siblings to follow hard after Christ. They lived a life of faith that was contagious.

Last of all, I dedicate this book to my many friends, who have made this all possible by their faithful prayers and financial support. Some of them have experienced these stories as they traveled with me. Others gave financially to make it all possible and prayed faithfully to make it a reality .

I am blessed beyond measure, and I give God all the glory for anything and everything that has happened through the ministry that He called me to. I pray that I've been faithful with what He put in my hands. My heart's desire is to use every available means to reach every available person.

This book is dedicated to my brother

Wayne Wingfield,

a pastor, an evangelist, one of my mentors, my friend,
my encourager.

He prayed for me!

He discipled many and equipped many to share their faith
as a way of life.

He left us far too soon!

July 7, 1937 – August, 20, 2022

ABOUT WINGFIELD MINISTRIES

~⌒~

The ministry began in 1981, operating as a part of Inter-Church, Inc., which was Dr. Myron Augsburger's ministry. As a student at Eastern Mennonite College, I directed crusades for Myron with the understanding that I would hire someone to direct my own crusades. We continued operating that way until Dr. Augsburger encouraged me to form my own ministry; he was not as involved in evangelism as I was, but he wanted to keep Inter-Church intact as his organization. So, Wingfield Ministries was formed.

Our emphasis was Encounters, crusades, and festivals, evangelistic events in communities smaller than those Billy Graham would go to, but doing basically the same thing that Dr. Graham did in larger metropolitan areas.

This was very successful for a number of years, but in the early 2000s, I began to see a change in our culture that affected our events. It was increasingly difficult to get unchurched people to attend; an event like ours was attracting a mostly Christian audience. Also, we had to get bigger and bigger names to bring in a crowd. I felt God had called me to be an evangelist and that paying so much for big names was not a good way to spend money. Then NASCAR opened up to us, and we began to go to NASCAR tracks and provide entertainment after the race along with the message of Christ. We've seen thousands of people make commitments to Christ over these last ten years. I'm thankful for that. Then COVID-19 hit in 2020, so for the past two years, we've been shut down and not able to go to tracks because the governors of various states would not allow large gatherings to take place. I hope and pray these doors will open up again in 2022, and we're planning on it.

We've also seen other changes in the ministry. For a number of years, we did galas centered around the book *Come to the Table*, and God used that in a significant way. Recently, the military outreach was birthed through our NASCAR events. Also, five years ago, God blessed us with the Lodestar Mountain Inn, and we moved to create a retreat to provide healing and hope for pastors and veterans. I'm very excited about what God's doing on the mountain. In 2022, we launched OneLife Institute, a gap-year program at the Lodestar Mountain Inn that gives kids thirty hours of college credit. I have requests from all around the world to come and do crusades, and I will continue to do that. Several requests have come from Africa and Romania asking me to come back and do evangelism and training. I was on a Zoom call this morning with over one hundred African pastors, and my topic was evangelism.

That's what has transpired since 1981 and what we're looking forward to. We have never lost focus on what God called us to do. I am an evangelist, and I am called to do evangelism and to equip others to do the work of evangelism. We need to use every available means to reach every available person. We just keep looking for new ways to do it. The gospel never changes but we need to continually look for new avenues to deliver the gospel message.